In The Damn Way

In The Damn Way

Life, Love, & Everything In Between

Brandy Alexander

Davion Alexander

TheRealBrandyAlexander

Contents

Contents

I dedicate this book to my sons. You gave me life when I was ready to give up. Love when I didn't love myself. Strength when the world beat me down. A voice when I thought I'd said it all.

Prelude

<u>Broken But Healed</u>

Have you ever met a man who tries to destroy your crown,
Tells you your nothing while he breaks you down.
Sit back and listen as I tell you how,
A man destroyed my heart and broke a vow.
A vow that he would love and protect me,
When his plan was only to disrespect me.
It all started when I was 14,
A girl looking for a love that she had never seen.
Fearless and gullible she was looking to fulfill,
The love that her life had forgotten to heal.
So, she met this boy who she thought was the guy,
Even though he had many flaws she was still eager to try;
To see if she could turn this boy into the man who would be her king.
A man who would one day give her, her crown,
A man who could turn her frown upside down.
You see she had prayed and prayed for God to fix these things,
But nothing was happening so he must be her fix.
Boy, boy, boy she must've been a lunatic.
It started with a slap, a choke, then a kick,
She's asking herself what is happening.
So, she said to herself maybe a baby would help
At 16, what in the world she's a baby herself
He didn't want a baby but he decided to stay
Because he was going to control her somehow some way
Physical was landing him in a place he didn't want to be
So, he changed his game to destroy her mentally.
He constantly played mad to confuse her thoughts
He made her believe without him she wouldn't last
He accused her of this and that because he wanted to control her fast
But one thing he didn't count on was her belief in God

BRANDY ALEXANDER

He even told her while he was in prison
Not to go to church because the men would hit on her which she
found particularly odd
So not only did she pray but she attended church when she could
She may not can quote the Bible but her faith she understood
And then one day as she was leaving a visit
She looked in her rear view and said this is it.
She took her kids and all of her strife
And on May 16, 2010 she took back her life.
In 2016 she started to love again
Telling herself this is nowhere near the end
So bit by bit she's continued to heal
Thanking God everyday because without him none of it would be real
And when he saw her again he couldn't believe his eyes
This woman had grown and she was unable to despise
The hate that he had used to attempt to break her down
Because unlike then she had truly come into her crown
You see she took back what the enemy stole from her
And restored her heart to bless those who needed her
And now she is able to tell her testimony
Something she's shared in whole with God only
Today is the day she tells that part of her life to take a hike
Because she's made it through that part of her life and God has said
it's time to drop the mic!

Foreward

Oh my gosh! I could not believe it. Not only had I finally spoken out about what happened in my life, I was able to share it. In 2022, I had been a part of the women's ministry for a while now. It was domestic violence month, and God said it was time. It was time for me to understand where he wanted to use me, but first, he had to make sure I was ready. The women gave me a standing ovation. Some of them would share their plight with domestic violence. We left church that day in a heaviness. There was more to be done; who knew it would begin with me.

Although I left church that day in heaviness, I was also excited. I accomplished what God asked of me. The next day, I received a text message from one of the ministers who was not in attendance. "Reverend" he wrote. "Who is reverend lol?" I responded. "I'm hearing that you PREACHED yesterday. Nah, the ladies said you did an awesome job yesterday," he responded. "They must be talking about someone else, lol. Oh well, that sounds better," I said, typing while trying to respond to text simultaneously, "Thanks to whomever said so. I definitely felt better afterward," I continued to say. "When are you going to write your book?" he asked "Lol, it's something I've said I want to do. Definitely have a story to tell," I said. "Stop sitting on your gift," he said. Those five words would snatch tears from my eyes. "I didn't know that was my gift. I've definitely been praying for God to show me what I'm supposed to do," I replied. "Encouragement is the gift. The book is the method," he stated. "I receive that, Minister, and I will definitely stop sitting on my gift. Thank you," I replied.

A book, really. How was God expecting me to write a book. I wasn't a writer. The more I thought about it, God was not tasking me to become a writer but to write, and the right people would help with the rest. Often, I felt like I was living a lie or living out someone else's dreams for my life. So, while I didn't know I was going to finish this project, I knew it needed to be done. People need to know the real Brandy Alexander and learn from all that I have experienced in my life.

{ 1 }

The Introduction

It was a hot summer's day in July 1985 when my parents decided to celebrate my birthday along with Independence Day. Selfishly since then I have never shared my birthday, but at this time I was out-voted. They settled on our back yard as the place to have the party. Oddly enough this was also the home where my father and uncle grew up. My great grandparents purchased this property in 1950 and after their deaths, my father and uncle abandoned it. The house was white and sat on about a quarter acre of land. There was an A on the front of it representing the "Anderson Family". Leading into the house were three cement steps with a chunk missing out of the second step. The screened porch was perfect when the weather was unbearable but cautious when company came because there was rotted wood. Unfortunately, this never stopped my parents from occasionally entertaining. Although the living room was small my dad and Ben built a wall size entertainment center that held my dad's many music vinyl records and the tv where he watched his favorite shows while eating dinner. Sometimes I joined him, and I was honored since it was the only time, he was still. During Christmas, my dad always made sure we had a real tree that met the ceiling at its peak.

Adjacent to the living room was my parents' bedroom. I loved to visit their room and play dress up from their closet that was filled with suits and dresses from their wardrobe. Ben's room was everything but what a teenage boy wanted for a room. His room was slanted and had a draft from the worn-down insulation that was hectic in the winter. It was just big enough for a twin bed and chest drawer. The den served a dual purpose as it's where we sometimes sat as a family, but it was also my bedroom. There was a wood stove next to the wall shared with the living room that was used to provide heat and sometimes cook on. My dad would have Ben reluctantly cut some of the many trees we had for wood. It was an open concept with the kitchen separated by a bar. The floor in the bathroom was very weak and as a result, the bathtub had to be taken out. The best part of the home was the front and back yard that were filled with Hickory, Pecan, and Black Walnut trees. If I wasn't climbing a tree, I would pick some nuts to crack. We also had a water well in the backyard that we used for water and to take baths. Although the home wasn't ideal for living in, but it was ours.

My parents met in junior high, and by high school graduation, they had welcomed my brother Ben. A year later they decided to get married as it was customary at that time. They bore another child, Angel, a year after me but she was stillborn. Deborah, my mom, is a beautiful dark skinned 5'2 woman with the most beautiful teeth and smile. She was sixth in a family of twelve children but the only child of her mom and dad. They moved to Charlotte from Shelby when she was young and, before long, met my dad. While Leslie, my dad, was a light-skinned skinny man who loved to show his teeth but suffered from overcrowding and a receding hairline that had started its triumph during high school. He was the seventh of seven children, with one being his twin who passed away as a baby. My dad was born and raised in Charlotte by his grandparents in the home we lived in. Although he and my mom were raised very differently, they shared a lot of traumas that neither one of them knew how to handle.

Before the big day, mama had gone downtown to Belk's and bought the prettiest pink pinstripe dress she could find. She pulled out the hot comb and as I jumped every time she came near me, straightened my hair so that I could have two pigtails. Each one was decorated with a white bow made into a barrette. As usual, she left out enough hair to make a bang, and after it was curled, she reinforced it with a pink sponge roller while I finished getting dressed. This look was mostly reserved for church, but today was special. While I was getting dressed, my dad came into the room, and after he planted a kiss on my mom, said how beautiful I looked. These words brought forth a smile a mile long. My dad was my everything, so his compliments always reign supreme.

After much planning and cleaning, it was time for the party. There was family and friends, clowns, games, music, and the grill going with hotdogs and hamburgers that everyone couldn't wait to chow down on. The gathering started attracting passersby from the neighborhood, which wasn't unusual. My dad had family and people he had known for years since he grew up here. When my mom announced it was time to cut the cake, I stopped playing so that all the attention was on me. Afterward, I opened my gifts and showed everyone what I had. There they were clothes, dolls, a big wheel, and some sunglasses my uncle had gotten from the Budweiser plant where he worked. After I hugged everyone, I returned to enjoy my playtime. Mostly, my time was spent with my brother, or tagging along with my dad, so playing was nice.

My mom had recently found out she was pregnant, and since I wasn't quite ready for school, she taught me from home. Since my dad worked the second shift, sometimes I would be outside with him as he cut wood for the cast iron we used for heat. Sometimes, my mom would use it to cook on. We had to be careful because you could easily get burned from it when it was hot. I knew from experience since Ben had come into the house jumping on a floor that was already weak, and a part fell off and burned my leg. This was where I took naps but was terrified after that. My parents were not big on going to the doctor, so they treated me from home. When it was time for her to deliver the baby, she left me with my great-uncle, who lived across the street until Ben got home. They were relatives of my dad's, and while he and his wife were nice, they were very frugal. So much so that he told me to eat cornflakes with water. When Ben got home, I was beyond ready to go.

Once we received the call that my mom had the baby, Ben and I caught the city bus over to Charlotte Memorial to see her. Many would say she was the most beautiful chocolate baby. Those big, brown eyes, shiny black curls, and a wide smile lit up the room. It was clear how happy my parents were, yet I couldn't shake the feeling that I was welcoming my new rival. They named her Camila, and over the next few months, the silent rivalry would manifest. One day I took her for a walk without permission and didn't know I had to buckle her in the stroller. As we attempted to go down the steps, she fell out. I'm not sure if this was an accident, but my tears proved convincing as they streamed down my face when they took her away in the ambulance. Red and blue lights faded into the distance. Left to console me was Ben.

Ben was a special guy in my life. He was 5'10, had the same big brown eyes as my sister, and a smile that looked like it should be the spokesman for a Colgate commercial. He was a natural athlete and, as such, played on the junior high and high school football and baseball teams. Educationally, he was just as elite, always landing a spot on the honor roll. Although we were nine years apart, we were besties as it was only us for years, and he was stuck babysitting most of the time. This was also during the time he became what people would refer to as a womanizer. Many girls without names would sneak in and out of the house when our parents left him to babysit. I never uttered a word. However, his secrets were exposed the day mom and dad caught him, unaware they would be home so soon. The entire neighborhood was spared from the screaming match between my dad and Ben. Their relationship was becoming strained now that he was getting older and wanting to live more like the boys his age. It was only natural since he was 14 and, because of money, never had the latest fashions nor was able to hang out because of me.

Their animosity was causing a great divide in our household. Secretly, my mom wanted all boys, so Ben was her first and favorite. So, when they argued, she was tasked with taking a side and silently it was always Ben. I was happy when the focus was shifted to me getting ready for kindergarten. My mom bought me some cute dresses and a new pair of black patent leather Mary Janes. This became my every-day wear that would eventually get in the way of me being a tomboy at recess.

What I thought school would be like and what it was were very different. I pictured this fun place where I made a lot of friends and learned a lot. It was more of a structured place that wanted you to be quiet the majority of the time. Because my natural ability was to be social, not speaking was one task, I failed plenty of times. The teacher constantly told me to be quiet or put me in time out for talking. Even though my dad praised us for our grades, I was equally scolded because I always received a "U" on refraining from unnecessary talk. My parents were two things' disciplinarians and educators, and right-fully so. Before I was born, my mom was a teacher at CPCC. Also, my dad was ex-military and raised by his grandmother, a teacher. When it came to school and misbehaving, if you didn't do your best at both, you were punished but rewarded if you did. Unfortunately, my flaw hindered me from receiving one of the crisp five-dollar bills my dad kept in his wallet to reward us for good grades. While this was heart-breaking, it didn't stop me from talking immediately.

Besides my parents, some of my classmates truly disliked me fre-quently feeling the need to speak to them when they needed to finish their work or take a nap. Some pretended to like me, but I could tell they secretly were jealous of my level of intelligence when I didn't fit into their level of hierarchy. They saw me as beneath them because I ate the free lunch at school and wasn't always dressed to the nines. It didn't matter because I had always been taught to be me. Besides, my real friends were waiting for me when I got home. My best friend, Trey, my cousin Carla, and Alisha all lived in my neighborhood, and until we went to school, there was nothing we lacked in my eyes. It wasn't until then that I felt I wanted to be something I wasn't, white. Now I wanted to have the lunch box, long straight hair, and listen to Bon Jovi. The fact that my life was good went out the door the minute I stepped into this classroom and was snubbed. So, while at school I pretended to be one of them at home I was accepted for me and that was the world I looked forward to.

Since mom worked as a secretary at our home church, New Zion Baptist Church, I would go there when I got out of school. Our pastor, Rev Jeremiah Robinson, was a wonderful preacher and a family friend. I enjoyed the sound of the typewriter as my mom typed up the programs, the smell of the xerox machine as the programs were being copied, and the taste of the candy that I would get from the pastor's candy bowl. Sometimes, my mom would let me help fold the programs. These were the moments I wished would last forever, but I appreciated them for what they were. At night, we picked my dad up from his job at Boise Cascade, where he was a forklift operator. Although my parents worked, we were living a very drab life, affecting everyone. Nonetheless, I was in awe of my parents and who they were in their respective lives.

The weeks were monotonous, with everyone doing their routines, but I lived for the weekends. Usually, this would be daddy-daughter time. My dad would wear a three-piece suit with a brim and some gators before we went to the local liquor houses. This was not my attire, as I was looking for someone to play with along the way. After I got my soda and snack, I let the grownups have their time unless no one was home, and then I was right beside my dad. It was always an honor to watch my dad charm the room with his loud talking and laugh to match. Sometimes, the family piled in our 1970 Chevrolet Impala on the weekends for an outing. While we were blessed to have a car, it had surely seen better days. It was brown, dented, and smoked, but it didn't matter when we were able to go to the Tik

House. Finding a parking spot was always a challenge so no one saw what you came in.

The Tik House was a small house on a dead-end street that was no bigger than some people's bathroom but a gathering spot for blacks to come see history being made. It was managed by my grandma and employed by my parents' family and friends. Afro-American baseball teams playing on the field, hot fish and chicken coming out of the wash pot, liquor and beer flowing from the house, and music blaring out of the juke box, this was the place to be. My cousins and I would get a pickle, pickled egg, or pickled pig feet and an ice-cold Chek soda and sing to Mariah Carey, Whitney Houston, and Karen White off the jukebox. Everyone knew who your parents and grandparents were, so you just ran around as a child without a care. From the outside, everyone appeared to have it all together, but the scandalous stories proved otherwise.

As I prepared to graduate from Kindergarten, I was recognized as academically gifted and instead of going to the first grade, I was placed in the second grade. Guess my talking finally proved to be useful. While I hoped this would help my influx of gifts for my birthday, I was wrong. My birthday came and went just like the rest of the days of the week. My mom was no longer working for the church and had instead taken a job with their previous landlord Cliff as his secretary. For Camila, this meant she would have to go to daycare and Ben, and I were now on our own. He became more resentful and started taking things like the car and my dad's favorite 49ers jacket to show it. Everyone was changing, and while they were struggling to get out of their current state, I watched it all unfold.

While my mom working was not only important to her but to the family, it was becoming an issue for us all. Because the car was no longer working, she was forced to catch the bus which meant she was home late. This meant dinner was late if at all and no one was there to see what Ben was becoming. He had begun taking solace in skipping school and hanging out over my grandma's house. Under normal circumstances this would have not been a problem except he was learning how to sell drugs. The money he was making was noticeable and as a result my dad put him out at 15. This meant I was back to Uncle David's house after school. Slowly my mom was getting home later and later and was sometimes being dropped off by a blue truck. The once quiet rumors of her affair were now becoming loud rumbles and starting to affect my dad. He was drinking more, and some said snorting cocaine that resulted in loud conversations to become dangerous arguments that we would have to leave home to allow time to recede. Although she denied it, I distinctly remember us going to a motel only for him to show up or her dropping us off at my grandma's so that she could leave with him. This man in this truck had picked us up as a family and taken us to the grocery store and now he was tearing us apart. So, at seven, when I saw my dad burning my mom's clothing, I understood. Eventually, I was able to stop him, but not before he chunked a nice heap.

Even though things were bad, they tried to put on a face as if everything was ok. It was if at the core they loved one another but not enough to stop their respective lives to fix their relationship. It wasn't until 1989 that the cracks that were being held together by scotch tape could no longer withstand the leak of lies, distrust, and infidelity that was pouring out. That Easter, after my mom picked us up, we stopped to see her boyfriend on what they called the "corner". The city had torn down some houses and now the local dealers, users, and locals used it as a hangout spot. Our Sunday's best was not ideal. I sported teal jogging pants with a yellow tank top, while my sister wore a grey sailor dress that somehow found its way out of a discounted store. Our hair was shaped and pressed by the bed we slept on the night before. We arrived home to crayons, markers, and coloring books scattered across the bed, fueling my excitement. While mom and dad dressed, I searched for our new clothes. Where dresses should have been only art supplies remained. Ben came home but just like us, he was met with nothing as well. Moments later, my mom emerged from her bedroom in a beautiful white dress dotted with flowers with her white hat, stockings, and kitten heels to match. Dad followed in his pink shorts, flowered shirt, black brim, and pink dress socks that were pulled up to meet his knees with dress shoes to complete his look. They were the image of Easter. We marveled at them as they posed for a picture, communicating with a smile that showed that our family was whole. This picture became the epitome of our family dynamic. That day was about as fake as that photo and the next day it was back to business as usual.

Over the summer, my uncle had to move in with us. This was his and my father's inherited home, so there was no denying him, even if he and my mom were rivals. It was never clear why they never got along but it probably had something with him being friends with the man in the blue truck as well. Uncle Eddie, Unk, was a 5'5", stocky, caramel skin color man with a receding hairline, but he always wore a bald head instead of my dad's favorite George Jefferson look. He'd spent time in the military but was honorably discharged and, since then, skated through life. He had two sons that I had spent time with years earlier but had separated from their mom. For reasons unknown, this meant separation from his children that for years was never spoken about. Now, he was with a woman who no one liked because of her nasty disposition. Unfortunately, he had put her on a pedestal, and that's where she resided.

Constantly, there was bickering about one thing or another, and it was becoming intolerable to be home. Unk had taken his position in the home and, to me, was overstepping boundaries. One day, I asked my mom if I could cook something to eat. She obliged and left while my uncle made it clear he disagreed. As he sat at the bar watching me cook, I could feel the disdain piercing through his big eyes. There was not much that I could cook, so I settled on bologna and eggs. They were horrible. You could see the grease sitting on top of the food and filling the empty spaces on my plate. To keep Unk from saying I told you so, I smiled like a chef reveling in their masterpiece while I ate.

When he turned his back, I attempted to throw out this feeble attempt at cooking an edible meal but was caught. As he sat there making sure I ate every bite, I imagined so many things I wanted to do to him. It didn't matter because I knew I couldn't, and if I didn't finish this food, it would be a problem. Angrily, I ate every bite until I finished what would be the worst food I've ever tasted.

After that, I made sure I stayed out of the kitchen and away from Unk if I could. Now, I had a new issue since my parents decided Camila and I should share a bed. She was a toddler now and nowhere near close to being potty trained. This family knew nothing about boundaries because every time I turned around, they were crossing one to make me uncomfortable. Not only had my dad and I stopped hanging so much, but now I was being peed on daily. As fall approached, our problems grew from my parents' marriage to the home we lived in being at risk. For weeks, meteorologists spoke about Hurricane Hugo, and how, it was tearing up everything on its path. Charlotte was next on the list to be affected, and no one in our neighborhood was prepared. That day, my dad and I walked to the liquor house before he decided it was time we go home. He felt this storm coming and was unsure how we would pull through. It was the first time I saw fear in my dad's eyes, but I knew him as my savior, so if he said we were fine, I believed him.

Our home was unfit for a light storm, so it was a scary night. The hurricane was said to have 90 miles an hour wind. It was snatching the hickory trees by the roots and slamming them down one by one beside our home. My dad told my mom if one falls on the house, you grab Brandy, and I'll grab Camila, and we're running out of the back door. It had been a while since I saw them come together as a team. Once daylight approached, my parents assessed the damage, and it was by God's grace that we were not struck. First thing the community did was make sure everyone was ok. Since we all lost power, everyone pulled together to ensure no one was hungry. As I looked out into the community, I hoped this was the beginning of us rekindling our family.

{ 2 }

The Beginning

Although the city had come through with its clean-up efforts, what had come before the storm was irreparable. Through the continuous disagreements she and my father had, she decided she would start her life on her own. To keep the peace, she got Unk's stepdaughters to walk me to what I found out later was my future. In a split second, my world changed, and no one thought it was pertinent to explain to me what was happening. None of my friends knew I was moving, and I didn't know that the last time I saw them was probably the last time. Tears filled my eyes when my mom picked me up from school the next day and told me that it was my last day. These last couple of years, my friends were the only thing keeping me company while she and my dad ran away from their responsibilities, and now, she saw fit to take that too. Anger filled my heart and mind, and I was certain to make sure she understood that.

Moving to Lakeview wasn't all that unfamiliar. Not only had we previously lived here, and Camila attended daycare here, but where she came to meet Leroy. Leroy was the man in the blue truck and now my greatest enemy. He was 5'10 with skin that mimicked those that were considered half Indian. Light skinned with fine hair also known as "good hair". He was a simple man who found joy in working and drinking with the boys on the corner or the local liquor house. His family was from South Carolina and his education was limited. Not the man I saw for my mom but the one she gave up her life to follow. He too was married and lived here with his wife. As we pulled up to what was our new home, I was not impressed. At first, I thought we were moving into a mansion, but I found out that this huge Carolina Blue house was three apartments. Her boss owned them and had allowed us to move in as a favor. The last time we lived here, my parents left owing debt so I guess we should have been grateful. We lived in what would have been the attic. There were about 30 steps that led to our apartment. God forbid something tragic happened because there was one way in and out. It was hardly big enough for one person, and here we had three. There was a small living room, kitchen, and bathroom, but the bedroom was the largest area, separated by a chimney that separated our bed from my mom's.

Mel lived across the street so at least I had someone to play with. Mel was two years older than me but was the only friend I had. Our parents had known one another a long time. Their home became the only place my mom allowed me to go so I was happy when Mel had to run errands because it was the only time, I was able to go somewhere. Her older sister Laticia and brother Jacob were protective of her and rightfully so. My mom quickly became overly protective and embarrassing. Certain places I would go, she would show up and tell me to come home for fear their actions would rub off on me. This would make complete sense if she was setting a better example for me at home. Almost immediately after we moved here, she became a different person all together. Her focused shifted to drinking more so that she could spend more time with Leroy. She became the talk of the neighborhood almost instantly because of how she erupted after drinking. Although most of the women were also sleeping with married men and hanging at the liquor houses, they never acted in such a way. This allowed them to point the finger at her and say, "do you see that, she has no class".

Leroy quickly made this his home away from home. Mostly, he came when he thought we were sleeping, but there were times he came during the day. She made sure to feed him when he came which made me want to throw my food away. Anything to show my disapproval, was how I spent my time. Whether it was kicking over tables or screaming how much I wanted to be with my dad, I wanted her to understand I didn't agree with this. Unfortunately, my mom was not here for me acting out nor did she care that I wanted my dad. As she stormed out of that bedroom to put me in my place, I immediately wished I had kept my anger to myself. Not only did she curse me and my dad for who he was, but she let me know that this was her house, and I had no say so. She was right. It was her house, and she could do what she wanted, so I had to find a way to get out of her house. Here I was, a nine-year-old child being spoken to like an adult because the sheet that served as the bedroom door revealed how much respect my mom had for her girls.

Jones Street was the heart of Lakeview, so while my mom was keeping me from people, just walking outside was plenty of exposure. The wine drinkers that stood on the stoop were sometimes arguing or fighting. For the most part, they only asked you for change as you walked to the store. In the beginning, I was afraid but, over time, I gained more courage. The streetlights were not helpful either, as some were busted in places where you could be attacked. We often ran past these parts or walked on the other side of the street. Nighttime was also when drug addicts and dealers plagued the streets. It didn't help that there were two nightclubs and a pool hall in and around the neighborhood. To top things off, there were a few liquor houses, and the main street was a prostitute highway. Coming from a community that felt safe enough to leave your door open all night to one where you never knew what would happen was an adjustment. When my mom wanted to hang out, she hoped we stayed in the house, but it never happened.

Tension and hostility best describe the relationship my mom and I developed. She was expecting a lot from me and producing very little. The loving, responsible mom I had grown to know was now living her life, leaving me to pick up the pieces for Camila. I had to pick her up from daycare, do her hair, and keep her while my mom was gone. I was grateful for Laticia when she asked if we wanted to learn how to cheer. Mel was uninterested so it was just me and I would find her once we were done. Who knew I would be a natural and it became an outlet for whatever argument my mom and I had for the day. Because Laticia was a cheerleader herself, she was able to show me the do's and don'ts to become a part of a squad. She introduced me to the coach for P.A.L. who was amazed at my skills and invited me to try out for the team. Unfortunately, when I needed my mom to show up for me, she couldn't and as a result I didn't make it to tryouts.

Although my mom and I had our differences, she was still my mom, and I loved her. Unfortunately, the love she was supposed to have for us constantly came into question. So, when I was awakened one night and told she was in an accident, my reaction was meh. I knew I was hurt because it was my mom, but because of what we had gone through, I was kind of relieved. She had gone from the loving mom I knew to this person who, for whatever reason, had a secret vendetta against me. Her prognosis was unknown, or at least they didn't tell us how bad it was. For two weeks, we went to stay with our neighbor, Barbara. She took very good care of us like we were her children. She had no kids, so this was just as good for her as it was for us. Our hair was done daily, we received new clothes, and slept in our own room. Going to school and being told you looked nice was a change of pace. There were no chores to be done and dinner was prepared daily. Ms. Barbara made sure that she got Camila from daycare, and I was allowed to play with my friends.

Finally, we were able to talk to my mom on the phone. She was ok but groggy from the pain meds she was given. I asked her what happened, but unfortunately, she had gone unconscious during the accident and couldn't remember. Later, we were told that the car went over a cliff, landed front first in a ditch, and subsequently split her leg in half. When she came home, I was crushed to see her in that condition. She had pins in her leg which limited her movements. The doctors placed her on bedrest until she began physical therapy. I was there doing whatever I could to make sure she was comfortable. My drive was lost when Leroy showed up to get what he needed and not do anything to help with things. WTF?! Here I was busting my butt to take care of her, and you come, and now she can do something, but it's to please you. Oh no, I was done. She could get someone else to help her I was not doing anything that I didn't have to do. Months passed, and slowly, she was able to get back on her feet. The injuries made it hard for her to work, which made our circumstances even more devastating. We never had much, so this was not new territory but not having much of anything to help made it that much harder. I did my best to recycle the clothes Barbara had gotten me, but it was no hope. We didn't own a washer and dryer which meant if you wanted some quickly you had to wash it on your hands. It was sometimes two weeks before we made it to the laundry mat.

As soon as my mom was "healed," she was back to drinking and partying as if this tragic event never occurred. Consequently, this took away my glimmer of hope that anything would change. I had enjoyed coming home to our house smelling like home from the food simmering in the kitchen. Finally, I was able to come home and tell her about my day. But we didn't move here for things to be better, so when the temporary mom gene passed, it was back to business as usual. While she was hospitalized, I figured out that she left my dad for the right reasons but found her freedom and was living in that moment. She was a mom and a wife before she was 18. There was no time for her to figure out who she was. The issue with that was that was not my problem. No matter what, I had done nothing to deserve anything less than a consistent good mom. Sometimes, I contemplated living with one of my relatives, but their situations weren't any better and were all in some way fighting the same battle. Besides, all I ever heard from them was negative talk about my mom anytime they were around. While many of them partied with her, they felt as if they were better than she was. Maybe it was because once my mom became inebriated, she cursed everyone. Nevertheless, finding someone to trust and look up to for guidance became harder and harder. Emotionally, none of them understood how their words cut, too. What child wants to hear someone speak ill about their parents, no matter how they felt about them. What was more hurtful about their actions is that I never heard my mom say anything about them.

Happily, after a long time coming, I was allowed to visit my dad. Since they needed time to discuss what I hoped would be a reconciliation, I visited the neighborhood to visit friends. This was what I needed. Not that I didn't enjoy the friends in our new neighborhood, but the vibe was different here. I could be me, and no one attempted to judge me. I enjoyed my tomboyish ways because they allowed me to have the best of both worlds. When I got into my groove, my mom said it was time to go. What?! How could this be happening again? Her words spoke volumes, and I deduced there was no reconciliation happening. After kissing him goodbye, I thought that the words she had spoken were true because he hadn't put up a fight. Unrecognized to them and me, their actions changed my innocence and, to this day, the way I feel about them. While no child should feel that their parents have fallen out of love with them, I did. Since Ben was finding his way through life and Camila and I couldn't get along long enough, I decided it was time to find a way to cope with my emotions.

Apparently, our lease was only for a year, and it didn't come soon enough. They say you must celebrate small victories, so while we were only moving downstairs to the middle apartment, it was worthy of a celebration. While it was still a one-bedroom, and Camila and I slept on the pull-out couch in the living room, it was better than walking 30 steps multiple times daily and having limited privacy. By this time the neighborhood that seemed so big was now small with what it had to offer. My plan for finding a way out was replaced with surviving. If I could just find a way to remove myself as much as possible, things would be manageable. Unk had moved to Winston-Salem and told me

I was welcome to visit anytime. He asked if I wanted to stay because he knew how my mom treated me, but I declined. It's one thing to be talked down to by your mom but his girlfriend was no better. Whilst she wasn't as brass as my mom, she had her way of sneering her face that turned me off from wanting to be around her much if any.

It was my last year in elementary and Camila's first year. At first it was cool with us going to the same school, but she had inhabited my mom's inebriated attitude but was too young to drink. She had become accustomed to me being at her beckoning call that she became irate the moment I didn't. Now she was old enough that when my mom said take her with you, I pawned her off on someone else or bribed her that I would bring her something back. I had come to Tuckaseegee Elementary late in the year the year before, so I spent that time getting adjusted. This year I was a "senior" so I wanted to do everything I could. Before I left Allenbrook, I was in a 4 & 5 grade combination class but that wasn't offered here. This meant most of 5th grade would be a breeze since I was already exposed. The chess club sounded nice, and it was for the two days my mom allowed me to go. She was responsible for getting me there at 7am but decided she wouldn't be doing that. Next was safety patrol but I didn't know enough people and was voted as an alternate. So, I just enjoyed my time and became my teacher's unofficial assistant which was a much better position.

Somehow my mom kept in contact with my dad and on graduation day they were both in attendance. While it was embarrassing to hear my dad holla imitating Arsenio Hall, I was happy to have him there. Soon after she allowed me to stay the night for which I gave her a big hug. My hope was I could convince my dad to let me stay. Before the move, we were "besties," and if I could explain to him how bad it was for me, he wouldn't hesitate to keep me with him. Then there was the horrible thought that he convinces me that living with my mom was better for me. While I didn't want to have to come back, I didn't want to be rejected either. At first glance, I could no longer recognize the family-oriented neighborhood. When we pulled up to the house, my dad wasn't home, and when we finally located him, I realized he was gone, too. Because Lakeview was full of dealers and activity, I knew the same epidemic had found its way to this country neighborhood, CRACK!

The light that had once shined in his eyes was now lost in the abyss of all the heaviness life had placed on his shoulders. The house was even more run down than when we lived there. It was hard to look at knowing how hard it must've been for my great-grandparents to obtain this home. There was no warmth, only the feeling of an empty shell. He was probably high at that time but had to put that aside now that I was there. I tried to smile, but honestly, I wanted to go home. I didn't know what happened, but all the furniture was gone except the couch in the living room that was now where my father slept. My guess was that he had sold everything he could and was barely getting by. It disgusted me that I had to go in a bucket if I needed to use the bathroom. While we were out, I made sure to use the bathroom so that I wouldn't have to know this feeling. For his "Bleups", my nickname, he did his best to put on a good front, and so did I.

Darkness fell, and I found out there was no electricity in his house. My mom's brother, who lived across the street, came and suggested I stay the night at his home since there was no electricity or running water. I would kindly decline. I felt as though they were judging him. Before we left Todd's Park, I had no memory of my uncle coming to my rescue. Why now? I wasn't here to judge what was happening around me. I was there to spend the night with the one person I knew loved me more than life. Also, I wouldn't dare make my dad feel like I didn't want to be there with him. He didn't speak on it as he probably knew my uncle was right for asking. We slept on the couch together, and he protected me with all his might and made sure I wasn't afraid. The morning came, and it was time to go home. Although I didn't want to be there either, it was a better alternative than this. My dad had this green bike that he gave to me after he used it to take me home. We stopped at the store along the way to get me some snacks as a substitute for breakfast. It was the most depressing ride. Not because I had to go back but because whatever was going on tore apart the strong man I knew as my father. The 15–20-minute bike ride felt longer since there was not much conversation. My mom and Camila came to the door when I arrived. He hugged Camila and extended my mom a casual greeting of hello. He stayed for only a few minutes before telling me he had to go. As he walked away to go home, I felt like he was walking out of my life, and in a sense, he was. While I wanted to fix my father all I could do was pray.

It was Summer of 91 when Unk decided to take Camila and me. I wasn't overly ecstatic about this, but I was willing to overlook my hesitations. Besides neither one of us had been out of town so this was an adventure. As we rode down the highway, I was amazed at the scenery only to pull up to what looked more country than Todd's Park. Winston-Salem was not a big city, and the anticipation was now towards the day we were going home. He promised fun but we only left with a fishing trip to brag about. Truly I was getting sick of the people in my life. The lies and broken promises were stacking up so high I could hardly see the truth. Before he left, he warned us that my dad had gotten a new girlfriend and it was not going well. Not only that but the house was being used as a crack house. My mom got a look on her face that I couldn't tell if it was of concern or victory. Either way I hoped she would take us to see him to make sure he was ok.

A few months later, my mom heard his new girlfriend had cut his throat and decided she needed to check on him. Realistically, this was none of her concern, but I was grateful that she took us with her to see about him. When we arrived, the place I called home was unrecognizable. There were people in and out the door and more in the yard. People I had never seen before. It was official that the house I once called home was now a crack house. Not only that but my father was now considered a crackhead to me, and that hurt. As I thought back to that time I stayed the night, I understood why I felt the way I did.

He was trying to cover it up, and my uncle knew what was happening the entire time.

My mom got out of the car hysterically, attempting to throw her weight around. Unknowingly, inside the house, his girlfriend, Norma, sat there, and she was not about to let my mom continue chastising my dad. Before a fight could begin, I jumped out of the car and grabbed my mom so we could leave. As a result of what I had just witnessed, I knew it was time I stopped longing for my dad. He was gone. Tears filled my eyes whenever I thought about what was happening, knowing I could do nothing. Unfortunately, I wouldn't be able to forget about the love I had for him, and each time I saw him, it showed.

In The Damn Way

Interlude

over time, I kept a diary of the subtle changes you made
when you spoke to me.
These thoughts grew limbs and proceeded to draw breath from my lungs
and a new thought emerged from the deflated remnants of flesh.
- this is where i die

~Davion Alexander

{ 3 }

Finding Me

The neighborhood changed quick as people moved out and new people moved in. Mel moved to Hoskins which was about a 15-minute walk from where we lived. Letitia had become a mom and could no longer coach me. It wasn't the first teenage pregnancy I had witnessed and was almost becoming a normal thing. My mom still wasn't allowing me to spend time with my cousins unless it was convenient for her. She kept me on punishment constantly to keep me from hanging with the older impressionable girls. Instead of teaching me the hard truths in life like teenage pregnancy, sex, or drugs, she condemned them personally while I defended who they were and not what they had done. This kept me defrosting refrigerators, scrubbing toilets or whatever demeaning chore she could find. It was hypocritical to watch my mom trying to keep me from everyone but herself.

While she attempted to keep me from my friends, she sent me into the lion's den. My aunt, who was complicit in my mom's shortcomings, was the one place I was allowed to stay. What she didn't know was my aunt deemed it beneficial for me to learn to be just like my mom. She taught me how to drink and I liked it. I began to look forward to our visits so that the alcohol could cloud my brain from my reality. While I was foolish enough to think this was love, she quickly showed me that in fact she was evil. She thought it was wise to divulge my insecurities to everyone that I wasn't developing as quick as everyone else. As I sat there while everyone laughed, I thought to myself that if I smack her would she still laugh. It was the last time I wanted to deal with her. Consequently, I went to another aunt's house that was even scarier. Her boyfriend fed us the alcohol and weed which by the way felt more wrong than what my aunt did. I learned these individuals were just as sick as my mom. Who had done whatever to them to make think this was ok? My mom never knew and because I enjoyed it, I never told her.

Every adult in my family had walked away from teaching us to be great men and women and turned into professors at addiction. While I reflect and say that would never be a relationship that I would have with any of my nephews or niece or little cousins for that matter, at the time, I enjoyed not feeling my pain. There was no care in the world from any of them, and I knew that. By this time, I truly felt that the person I was or wanted to become would not be accepted in this climate. While looking for someone to look up to, I realized that I would have to pick someone and go for it. No one was discussing college and becoming teachers, congresswomen, bankers, or even doctors. They discussed getting to Freak Nik, whatever club was popular, dating the guy with the most hood money or being that guy. When I say hood money, I'm referring to being a hustler, however that may look. As I admired them at that time, I saw that none of them making it out of the projects, but they were all I had. My parents stressed the importance of education and the opportunities it brought, yet by this time, they both were failing their teachings. Unfortunately, the people in my neighborhood were of the same practices and outcomes. It was as if life was telling me to pick a place and stand because this was as far as I would go.

10 years old and I was already becoming a rebel. It started with cutting and relaxing my hair and more sneaking around whenever possible. Mel's mom and my uncle were in a relationship so when my cousins visited their dad more, I was happy. It gave me more of an excuse to walk the 10-15 minutes to Hoskins to visit with them. Mel

and I were still close but when they came over my focus shifted. Letitia was still in Lakeview so when I could I hung out with her for a while. Now that she was a mom, things were different. Especially since her baby daddy mimicked my future husband. That summer Unk thought it worthy to bring both my sister and me to Winston-Salem. I don't know if my mom had anything to do with it now that Camila was old enough to cause more trouble. Either way it was a peaceful week as there was nowhere to go so nothing she could tell. We both allowed curiosity to take over as we snooped through his girlfriend, Mary's things and found out that the long hair she praised was actually a weave. He may have kept her on that pedestal, but I was finally able to see who she was.

Once we returned my mom surprised us that we were moving. While I hoped for a new house with a yard outside of Lakeview away from Leroy, it was across the street. Some people are reluctant to change, but my mom made sure we understood that it was inevitable. While I thanked her for continuing to try to give us a decent place to call home, I would have enjoyed having that one place. It was a lot better than where we were. It was a brick, two-bedroom, townhome apartment. The complex was small with only eight apartments that formed the shape of an L, with four on each side. There was no grass to play in as the front yard was a concrete parking lot. However, a small area in the back housed a clothesline for each apartment. Although we shared, I was excited that my sister and I had our room. Over time, I saw there was something weird about these apartments. Most people who moved in were single women with children. The time they spent there was never long, and this I couldn't understand. No more than I understood why we were always moving. I found out later that the mothers of these families were fighting their own demons, and so they were doing the best that they could. The one thing I respected is that even though they were going through things, they made time for their children's lives. By the time I made new friends, it wouldn't be long before they were gone.

I did meet one person who became a long-time friend to me. Her name was Emily, and she became my best bud. She moved here from Paw Creek; wouldn't you know it; our parents grew up together. We endured so much of the same pains that it was destined for us to connect over trauma. Although she was enduring pain, she had sisters who were there trying to pick up the pieces. She was into sports just like me, so we had fun outside of life's troubles. She invited me to her softball game once, and she also played basketball. I wasn't good at either, so I continued to cheer. We spent a lot of time just hanging out. As a child, you have blinders, and if you're not careful, you keep them until adulthood because you learn it's easier to act like you don't see what you see. Emily was clear as to what was happening in her household and had become immune to it. I didn't see that the doors I was walking in for love were imploding with drug use and dealing. The issue for me was that I could feel the conversations being held as I was walking up but to blind to see what was happening in my home. I leaned on Emily to escape the people who laughed at me instead of with me. When her sisters would come to rescue her, I waited for my brother Ben to do the same, but it wouldn't happen. As a result, I learned how to be fake and pretend I was ok when, in fact, I wasn't. I felt more love when I could go with Emily around her family than I ever felt at home. We discussed our dreams and how we wanted to get out of this messed up life, but life had its way of laughing at your plans, and it certainly would. For now, my plans were to keep my blinders on and move through life until I found a way out.

Summer was over and it was back to school. My first year of middle school. I was nervous and excited at the same time. Because school assignments were based on neighborhoods, I was familiar with many of my classmates, but I also met some new faces. Some of them I later called friends, and others just people I knew. The setup for middle school was different. Every grade level was on separate wings. Each wing was divided into "A and B" teams. The only time we integrated was during electives. Although you spent core classes with the same people, I looked forward to electives so that I could be with my friends on the other team. Mel had gone to the same school and taught me a lot of what I was learning, so I was ahead of everyone else. She made everything sound so amazing that I was ready to experience everything.

The funny thing about self-esteem is that you don't know how much you don't have until someone does something really degrading, and you keep them in your life. As a preteen with no emotional stability and two parents who had checked out, I developed a bad case of low self-esteem. Some think that you walk around with your head down, wanting to kill yourself, but in my case, it was a need for acceptance. When you have experienced not being wanted by your parents, you start to yearn for it from whomever. I sought some of my needs from a boy. One who probably was seeking some help from a girl like me. Psychologists would say I had daddy and abandonment issues, and they would be right. I was 5'2, brownskin, super skinny with broad shoulders and calf muscles strong enough to kick a horse and knock him out so I didn't look like the other girls. Also, I was the president of the itty-bitty titty committee. Before moving here to Lakeview, it didn't matter. My friends and I usually climbed trees, fought, or raced one another. No one was worried about how I looked, but I was faced with my flaws, and I didn't like what I saw. Maybe that was because it was the butt of many jokes from those who claimed they loved me.

So, when this guy approached me, I thought he would be my savior. Anthony began a long history of me looking for what I needed from the wrong guy. He was new to the school, so all the girls thought he was the best thing. Honestly, he was just as broke, busted, and disgusted as many of us were. Once he asked me to be his girlfriend, I was privy to who he really was, and I wasn't impressed. He was only interested in putting notches on his belt, so we didn't date for long. Even if I were ready for sex, he wasn't the one I wanted to take that journey with. His way of breaking up with me was accusing me of someone else right before he slapped me in the face. It was the most cowardly move

I've seen, but that's how those types of guys act. Although I was hurt by how he did it, inside, I was happy that he could no longer continue making a fool of me. He lied so much about who he was and what he had to prey on girls whose self-esteem was already low. Eventually, he moved through my so-called friends even though I tried to warn them. I didn't want to be this person. At first, I was confused and wondering how I got to this point. What was it about having a boyfriend that was so important now? Then I realized that it was being shoved down my throat by every woman I knew. No matter how bad he was for you, you had to have a man. That's not to blame them for my poor choices. I'm to blame for shaking my head at what I saw yet mimicked in my life.

Fall came and sports were in full swing. Halfway through the football season, there was a pep rally for drug awareness. As a tribute, we were tasked with writing about the subject. It was befitting as I'm sure there was more than me dealing with someone, they knew who was addicted to drugs. It was supposed to be a letter to a friend talking about how drugs were affecting their life and pleading with them to get help. Who knew that what I had written would become real life. It hurt my soul to later see a friend of mine addicted to the one thing we both shook our heads at trying to understand how someone could do that. Our dance teacher told us we would be performing as well. I invited my mom as this was the first time, I had won a contest and would perform in front of a large group. I practiced with all my might, hoping she would surprise me by showing up. Unfortunately, she wouldn't make it, but I didn't let that steal all the hard work I poured into this. Everything I feared didn't happen. It was true; I was exceptional at everything I put my hands to, but I had no one to push me to do more. If anything was going to happen, I was going to have to surpass my fear and trauma so that I could excel. I stopped focusing on having a boyfriend and started believing in my capabilities and how I could grow them.

In The Damn Way

At the time, I didn't understand God and how he worked, but as I recollect those days, I understand that he was always with me. Whenever I tried to go left, he would pull me to the right. Sometimes God would win, and I would go right, but it was staying to the right that showed to be my problem. One day, as I was walking down the hall, I stumbled upon something I had been waiting for an opportunity to accomplish. It was a sign that read, "Cheerleading tryouts next week". An opportunity to be a part of something bigger than my small world. Would I be good enough? I was taught by one of the best. We had practiced and perfected who I needed to be as a cheerleader, but I was up against some true talent. The girls who were already on the squad were fierce. They had started with P.A.L. and were the best on the Westside. Unbeknownst to us, they hired a new cheerleading coach, Ms. Avery. She was a member of the sorority AKA (Alpha Kappa Alpha) and a college cheerleader looking for fresh talent that could move from P.A.L. cheering to outright elite cheering. Her vision for our squad was precision, tight formation, enunciation, and leadership that would win us cheering competitions. Yes!

Letitia had already given me the blueprint to be a great cheerleader. I just had to add what this coach wanted from us and kill it. We learned spirit fingers, wrist formation, and, most importantly, how to create your voice for cheerleading. My goal was to be recognized, and I was consistent. My self-esteem was climbing because this world was befitting to my personality. I ensured my moves matched by going home and continuing to practice. The previous cheerleaders were not here for the changes but stayed, thinking they would automatically make the cut. They would be on the activity bus voicing their complaints, and I kept to myself. I was just excited about being able to try out and focused on making the team. Finally, Friday came, and it was cut day. We did our individual skills before performing with our assigned group. Afterward, we were asked to sit in the bleachers at the gym. One by one, we were called down and crowned the cheerleaders for the 92-93 school year. The anticipation was worse than the tryouts.

Sitting and wondering if you had done enough to be a part of this unique group preparing to do more than cheer at football and basketball games. Just when I thought I was not chosen, Brandy Anderson would be called. OMG!! I hollered! Finally, my new potential was being noticed, and I would not let them down.

Once we were all selected, we were introduced as the new cheerleaders of Wilson Middle School. Not one of the previous cheerleaders was picked for the new squad. The ladies were devastated. It was hard to celebrate when they didn't make the team. Some that made the team couldn't cheer anywhere near as good as them, but that wasn't the point. We had to be able to leave that entitled attitude of just being good because where she was taking us had no room for that. The gym doors opened, and my mom was there waiting for me. This was a memory I will never forget. I ran and fell into her arms, crying so much. She asked me, "Brandy, what's wrong?" and I replied, "I made it. I made the team." She asked, "Why are you crying?" to which I replied, "I'm so happy". It had been a long time since I was genuinely happy, and it was overwhelming.

During that time my dad had made his way to live with Mel and her family in Hoskins. When I learned that my dad was hiding out there, there was no question that I was going. I chose to deal with the consequences later. In just a little under three years, I watched this man go from strong and confident to weak and withered. The suits were gone, and decent clothing was a luxury. I still remembered how he bragged while singing Johnny Kemps "Just Got Paid" on Thursday nights as we went to the liquor house because it was payday. Now he was constantly in between jobs. I found out he was at my uncle's because of some unfortunate misfortunes. While I was ecstatic about seeing him, he didn't reciprocate the same reaction. Maybe he was embarrassed about seeing me in that way. Word on the street was that some young boys jumped on him just because they thought it was funny. Although it hurt me deeply, I refused to allow him to see me in that vulnerable emotion as he didn't deserve to. Unfortunately, I made a terrible decision to embarrass my dad even more in hopes of getting back at him for how I felt. As my cousins and I were walking back to my neighborhood and my dad was walking to the store, I yelled at him to be careful as some young boys were at the store. He gave a chuckle, but my cousin nudged me and stated that was wrong, but I shrugged my shoulders. Inside, I was kicking myself, but I never let it show. Not long after, Unk told me that my dad had lost the house and was in Winston Salem.

Learning that my dad was really gone without so much as a good-bye was a gut punch. If it was what I said, then I wanted to apologize. Unk reassured me it was so he could be helped. Instead of my life improving there were more hurdles being placed in the way of my happiness. Questions were beginning to form, such as, why was this happening to me? What did I do to cause this? And would anyone miss me if I was gone? It helped when I could hang with my cousins but that wasn't always an option. Just being one of the girls and not wondering what anyone thought was better than getting upset and possibly fighting because of how you are dealing with life.

I made what would become my last summer vacation to Winston-Salem in hopes of seeing my father making his combat. Only to find that he was gone because his drug habit had escalated to him stealing from Unk. As I was drowning in sorrow I met Norma's daughter, Tish who was able to understand my pain. It was the first time I could be open and honest which felt great. She too would become a distant memory until later in life.

{ 4 }

Losing Me

There is a quote by an anonymous writer that stated, "stay positive and keep believing, better things are ahead". This was my stance as I was entering 7th grade. Now that things were manageable, I regained some of my self-esteem. Cheerleading was very demanding with practice being four days a week over the summer. All our hard work paid off, and we were ready for the season. I could also choose what electives I wanted, which broadened my reach even further. Alright! This was my time to shine. All of these were something I was either good at or could learn. I set a goal to be happy and the best at everything I signed up to do. Later, I attended tryouts and was selected as a part of the dance team S.W.A.T (students with a tude), learned how to sew and cook, painted my first masterpiece, and created my first ceramic pottery fish. The ceramic pottery fish later served as an ashtray, but I was just excited to accomplish something outside of what I knew. Physical education exposed my athletic abilities, which proved to be pertinent later.

As school was back in session, our practices were after school but not welcomed by all. The previous cheerleaders were still upset they didn't make the team. Sometimes, they showed up just to show their disapproval. Eventually I understood, but before now, I didn't know how much this meant to them. My goal was not to dwell on it. One night after practice, we were all on the activity bus, and some girls were discussing their grievances. Cheerleading was all some of them had. They had come from broken homes and being on the squad brought them joy. Wow! From the outside, looking in, I saw that these girls had it all. They were beautiful, well-dressed, and popular. How was their self-esteem an issue? How was it that these girls were experiencing the same pain that I had emotionally and mentally? It was through this that we evolved into friends instead of enemies. From that day forward, these ladies became cheerleaders for the cheerleaders.

Soon, the coach invited us to bring new material to the squad. This was it! Emily and I were always coming up with dance and step routines, so we joined together to develop something fierce. This opportunity was a confidence boost for me. Not only were our ideas chosen, but Emily and I were asked to teach the girls the steps. This became my position in the squad. Before long, people came to the games to see us cheer. It was like a scene out of "Bring It On". Our team wasn't that good, but our cheerleaders always beat the silent rival between the opposing cheerleaders. It was more exciting than watching the game. I did my best not to worry about home as it would be what it was. All I yearned for was to see my mom come to support me at one game or more, but unfortunately, she was unable. Because of her new lifestyle choices, she was deduced to cleaning for some guy my uncle introduced her to, who gave her access to the company van. This meant on the nights I needed a ride; she used it to pick me up, which was embarrassing. I focused on the positive that at least I had a ride, and she was working.

Slightly, I began to notice a guy staying after school who wasn't playing sports. Now, I never said I wasn't into guys anymore; I just stayed away until he caught my eye. He never said much, so I didn't know who he was or what he wanted, but the girls and I checked him out anyway. One day his friend Carl walked up to me and told me someone liked me in the eighth grade. What?! I knew some people, but not any who wanted to be in a relationship with me. I asked him, "who?" He said, "Aaron" Aaron, I didn't know any Aaron. I was mind-boggled for days trying to figure out who he was. It wasn't until we were introduced that I realized he was checking me out this whole time. I couldn't understand why, as even though I was cute, the other girls had better clothes and kept themselves nicer than I was. Now, I wasn't a slum, but let's face it, we didn't have the latest or greatest or anything close to it. This left me questioning why me but made me fall head over heels that someone like him wanted someone like me. I know what you are thinking, you are 12 years old. What are you talking about? Until you have put on these shoes, you cannot begin to fathom what this meant to me. He was very slim, around 5'5, with a deep voice and a caramel complexion. We instantly became inseparable. Although we were on different halls, made sure to walk me to class and the bus even if it made him late. Several times, he almost missed the bus, but that never stopped him.

It wasn't long before Aaron began staying after school to ensure I was good. It was sweet. He was coming to each practice and sneaking to ride the activity bus home, as it was only for athletes and those with notes for afterschool activities. None of which applied to Aaron. He would also stay for home games and make sure I wanted for nothing. Finally, I had someone that supported me, and that was all I could ask for. At one game, I did a spread eagle at halftime, but landed incorrectly and twisted my ankle. Not only did he ice my ankle during the rest of the game, but he also got off the bus with me, made sure I got home, then walked home. This was unbelievable, especially since all we had done was kissed. After he was caught a few times and threatened with suspension, he decided to try out for basketball to continue riding the activity bus. Don't get me wrong, I supported him fully, but this was not a good idea. Aaron was not what you would call athletic nor, did he have the build for a basketball player. This was a time of baggy clothes, and I was caught off guard because I had never seen him without a shirt. OMG! Let me just say he must've cared a lot for me.

As our relationship grew, it was only right we met each other's parents. I didn't want him to meet my mom as I could never tell her mood, but he was thrilled for me to meet his. So much so that he invited me to Thanksgiving with his family. Not only was I nervous but I had a stomach virus the week before and had no clothes appropriate for meeting my boyfriend's family. Mel let me borrow a yellow, short-sleeved ruffle shirt with a white sweater, which I paired with blue jeans and Sam and Libby loafers. Yes, I know! My outfit was out of season, but it was the best I had, and I wanted to impress them. This was the first time a boy had come to my house, and he was a gentleman. He came in to get me, and that was the only time I let him meet my mom. She hadn't been drinking, so it was okay, but I rushed along the meet and greet so we could go. You could tell he was nervous too, but he gave nothing but respect as they were introduced. After I allowed her all of two questions, I signaled that we needed to get going.

The ride to his family home was the longest, although it was only 15 minutes from where I lived. When we arrived, I was astonished. Everyone greeted me with smiles and hugs just before the women went inside and the men outside. Aaron came inside after a short while to sit with me. He wanted to make sure I was comfortable, and I appreciated him for that. Not only that, but he also offered to fix my plate because he knew I was nervous. He and his family were everything I wanted and needed in my life. Although we used to be a family once, I had never experienced this type of environment. There was no cussing or drunkenness. There was only laughter and love with his grandma, who set the tone for the environment. Was I in a dream? Aaron and I stayed together until that unforgettable spring day.

Cheerleading season was over, and I'd decided to run track. I ran the 4x100m relay, 100m relay, and did the high jump. Ms. McVey, our coach, made us unstoppable. When I tell people I did the high jump, they look at me with disbelief because I am 5'2" but I was very good. Aaron continued to support me, but it never stopped me from hoping my mom would make it to at least one meet. By spring it was time for the eighth graders to take their annual Carowinds trip. Aaron had been a gentleman thus far, so I had no reason to have any fears. While I missed him and our walks to class, I manage to stay occupied. However, during breakfast the next day, the same friend who introduced us told me that Aaron was coupled up with his ex-girlfriend. All his friends were in the eighth grade and in relationships with other eighth-grade students, so they were all coupled off on rides. Pretending was one thing, but he proceeded to tell me that they kissed. I was upset. I wanted it not to be true. Especially since it was coming from a "friend". What friend would do that? He had to be lying.

After I approached Aaron, and he truthfully admitted to the accusations my whole world seemed to fall apart. The entire day, I tried to understand what I had done to make him hurt me like this. Aaron tried to talk to me, but I wasn't ready to receive his explanation. It wasn't until it was time to go home that I allowed him to explain. As I stood there ignoring his side along with an apology, I turned red and as a result slapped his face. This was the end of Aaron and me. What's crazy is I was with Anthony, who cheated and said nothing but couldn't take this one incident from Aaron. I would say now that I expected that from Anthony because I knew he wanted a name for himself and was just as lost as I was. Aaron, on the other hand, had more potential, and I expected more from him. He was husband material, not a clown, but now he was right there with the clowns. Later, he became a replay in my mind as I tried to see what my life would have become had I stayed. As track season came to an end, I rallied around the fact that we were first in our division. Cheerleading tryouts came again, and of course, I made the team, but it wasn't as good as the first time.

By the last few weeks of school, I was holding in so much anger and resentment that it wouldn't take much to set me off. Nikki had moved into Lakeview a few months before and I did my best to befriend her. As I introduced her to my cousin, Sharon I hoped they too could become friends. Sharon was not as gullible as I and could see through this girl, but I brushed it off. Wouldn't you know it, that Monday Nikki thought it would be funny to joke about my cousin. When I confronted her to say that to Sharon's face, she played it up to the crowd and obliged. Now, I don't know about anyone else, but my cousins were like sisters to me. It wasn't enough to fight over in school, but I knew this wouldn't end well for her. Just so happened my cousin was over that weekend, and I made sure I made her aware of what was said. Immediately she wanted to confront her, and I was intent with showing her the way. As she walked out of the house and saw Sharon you could see the fear in her eyes. Of course, she tried to weasel her way out as most cowards do, but my cousin knew I wouldn't lie. All I could do was laugh because just a few days ago she was hard as a rock. She let her know that the next time wouldn't be so generous as we walked away.

That Monday she was one way to plot her revenge against me. Unfortunately, she knew she was no match, and she possessed no allies at home, so she sought after ones at school. What she said to get them involved I'll never know but it was definitely a manufactured beef. They too misjudged my size and demeanor.

Days leading up to the brawl, she repeatedly tried to intimidate me, but I let it slide. She was beneath me, and I wanted her to know that. Finally, they worked up the courage to approach me. To make sure they had an audience to cheer them on, they made sure to tell anyone that listened. Some of my classmates thought it wise to warn me of the rumors. What they didn't know was I overheard the whispers and anticipated their retaliation. As we left Art class and went through the double doors of the main hall, I heard my name being called. "Brandy, since you got all that mouth, let me see what you have to say now", she said. "OK" I replied, seemingly unbothered by what was happening. The crowds had begun to gather along with those passing through going home for the day. I didn't know, but they were surrounding me. I had tunnel vision on the one that started this whole thing. Once we were on the ground, because one was pulling me from the back and we all fell, I began hitting her harder. Someone told authority and they were on the way, so the guys pulled me off and told me to leave. I walked right past the principal who didn't know I was the one fighting. Tears of anger and emotion were falling but I didn't make a scene. Celebrating that I got off unscathed was ended when I was asked by the principal to step off the bus. From the bus and into the principal's office I went.

There they were: Larry, Curly, and Moe sitting there with a stupid look on their face. I was furious. One, because this was now on my record, and two, at least, be the one to win if you decide to jump someone. Although they were disappointed in my actions for fighting, they understood the circumstances, and I received in school suspension instead of out-of-school suspension. Whew! I had never experienced either, but if I could come to school, no one had to know what happened. In school suspension (ISS) kept me on track for perfect attendance which was awarded with two tickets to Carowinds. That didn't last long because I had to call my mom to pick me up from school. She wasn't happy but gave me a pass this time since I was provoked. The next day, the fight was all everyone wanted to talk about, but I just wanted to get my day done. I wasn't a bully, nor did I like to be bullied into anything. To be pulled into a fight that was unnecessary and proved absolutely nothing was not a conversation I wanted to continue to have.

The last day of school finally arrived; as luck would have it, I missed the bus. My mom's car needed repairs and no one else owned a car. She had also quit working the cleaning job so the van was gone too. Nikki also missed the bus, so I was tasked with asking if I could hitch a ride with them. Having to ask if I could ride in the same car as her was a test of my patience, but if I wanted to get my Carowinds tickets, I had to suck it up. She still had a nasty disposition that I had to humble myself to receive for the 20–30-minute ride to school. As I sat in the back of the van, I could feel her rolling her eyes and thinking what she wanted to but dare not say. It wasn't an easy ride, but I kept my eyes focused on the scenery as we drove up Tuckaseegee Rd. Later that day, I was told that Nikki told people she talked junk during the ride. I wanted to slap the taste out of her mouth again as I saw she hadn't learned anything. I made out lucky the last time with no suspension, and besides, no matter what, she would always be that person you wanted to slap, so I let her talk. Finally, it was the last day and as I received my awards with my tickets I laughed at this year and hoped next year was better.

Over the summer, I was able to forget most of the crazy things that happened during the school year. Now that there was no Aaron and Nikki was less than a thought, I focused on who would accompany me to Carowinds. While I planned so did my mom and surprised us with an impromptu vacation in Virginia. Her older brother, Pop, settled there after he retired from the military. All I knew about him was he came home sparingly and was the one that "had it all together". We all looked at them as model citizens but even the cleanest garment has a blemish. Why we were going there I could never understand but packed my most decent and off we went.

One thing I can say about my mom is she never kept a man in her life that she couldn't use for something. Unfortunately, as a preteen looking at this, I wondered what she was doing. As we snuck away to take that drive to Virginia with the "friend", Richard, Camila and I snickered in the back as he begged my mom to be with him. He probably was a better option for her, but she was uninterested. When we arrived, I was in awe of the scenery. Nice homes, large trees, and air as fresh as a crisp winter morning. A suburban life that I had never been introduced to but one I quickly knew I wanted. We stayed for two weeks, and for that time, we were a family again. No drunkenness and arguments only love from my mom as we took walks and had much-needed talks. This was what I envisioned when she told me I was never going back to Todd's Park. He offered her a life here with help to get her on her feet. I'm still perplexed as to why she didn't take it and why I was in such a rush to come back.

At that time, my only concern was the huge party I would have once we got back to Charlotte. Surely me turning 13 warranted a party but that was only a thought I possessed. Before we left, my aunt took my mom to get me a few things and took us all to the beach. This was my first beach vacation. I visited the beach on a school trip but wasn't allowed to get in the water. It was beautiful and just for a moment I forgot I wanted to go home.

Sitting on the beach, I thought about why this couldn't always be who my mom was. Why was our world filled with so much chaos? Maybe this was her opportunity to fix things by permanently making Virginia our new home. Of course, I wanted to get back to my friends. This life had been forced down my throat, and now that I had become accustomed to it, it was hard for me to leave. I don't know her reasoning for deciding not to take it, but two weeks were up, and we were on the way home. I was excited as my birthday was in a few days, and I had earned a party or at least the opportunity to use my Carowinds tickets. I enjoyed what suburbia had to offer and was happy and sad to leave it behind.

When we arrived home, I was excited to see the streets of Lakeview. I was too young to understand how these streets were tearing my family apart and that we were better off where we were. I was eager to tell everyone about how much fun we had and get ready for my birthday. My mom spoke honestly when she said I had already had my birthday celebration. Not even a cake. I also had to put my certificate and tickets in a bin with the rest of my awards because she wasn't taking me to Carowinds either. Unfortunately, it was time I took my head out of the clouds and realized what life was shaping up to be. If I learned anything by this point, it was that the people in my life were hell-bent on disappointments when it came to me. Not that I was ungrateful for the Virginia trip, but I didn't ask for that. I was no longer meant to be happy if they had it their way. I had to pay them back for the one birthday party I had ever seen them have for me for the rest of my life. Someone has said I was spoiled as a baby, I remember, so maybe that was my debt. I don't know what it was; all I know is that they made sure that they collected it. Consequently, I learned to suppress my hurt and anger so far inside that it was sickening. I couldn't be disrespectful because I was too afraid of the consequences. I couldn't leave because I had nowhere that I could go. All I could do was pray and hope that one day, God would answer. Until then, I lost interest in what used to make me happy.

There was a glimmer of hope. Ben, unbeknownst to me, had fathered a child that was born four days before my birthday. He brought him over to introduce him and verify he was his child from my mom. This was something for the courts to do but for whatever reason he ran to his mom. From the moment I saw him I knew he was my brother's child. Hell, he looked like he could have been my child. Instantly, I fell in love with BJ as he was the only one, I trusted to love me. Unfortunately, this created a wedge with Missy as she was not BJ's mom. They tried for months to embrace his birth but inevitably she put him out.

Shortly summer was over again, and it was back to the hustle and bustle of education. Now I was a senior in middle school but had no more than when I began two years ago. My uncle promised to get me some all-white Nike's for school but reneged. My mom took us to the 7-dollar store to find the least expensive two outfits, PayLess for shoes, and off we went. I tried not to be so bummed out, but everything was starting to get to me. I tried my best to put on a smile, but inside, it was as if life had been sucked out of me, and all that was left was a hollow shell. Although cheerleading was the one thing bringing me any type of satisfaction, I had lost the fire inside of me for it as well. It wasn't just me who was feeling the blues. Ms. Avery no longer brought the enthusiasm and fierceness from her love of cheering. Something was happening in her personal life, and it was spilling over. She had become that mom figure for me at this point, but she was in no position anymore. It wasn't long before I put her in the group with every other person who said they would be there for me. I decided to quit the team, although she'd asked me repeatedly to stay. There was nothing more for me here, and besides I wanted to be home with my new boyfriend.

Shockingly, my mom decided we were moving before I could get this going. This time, it was out of the neighborhood and across town. What?! I started to wonder were we running from something or to something. Once again, I left everything and everyone behind and started a new life in a new school and neighborhood. The good thing about it was I was closer to family, although my mom didn't allow me to go anywhere, so this meant nothing in hindsight. I hoped to get on the cheerleading squad to find some normalcy, but they already had tryouts and were reluctant to add me to the team. I didn't understand that this was the worst move of them all. The enemy had come into my house and was there to stay a while.

On the other hand, we finally moved into a house. It was on West Blvd. directly in the path of the animals headed to the Coliseum when the circus came to town. While it was a small, white, two-bedroom one bath house, there was a barn in the back yard. There were no drug dealers dealing right on the side of my house now, but we heard traffic constantly. This was the major pipeline headed to the Airport and several housing projects and low-income neighborhoods. One thing I learned is that my mom sure knew how to pick them.

As usual this was the party house. The weekends were filled with people and the endless flow of liquor until my mom got ugly. My feelings about what was happening were invalid. No one cared to listen, so I bottled up how I felt about this new place, school, my parents, and my mental health. As a result, I begin to become reclusive and walking down a dark path. I chose to be alone because it felt good. I was taking any kind of pill that put me in a coma to get through my school day. It wasn't anything new as I used some of these pills for medical reasons, but now it was recreational. Even Camila took on a new persona that took my mom from her job to her school almost daily. No one gave a second look at what I was doing. Most days,

I only contemplated taking my life until one day, I tried. Replaying one the many inebriated arguments I had with my mom, I grabbed a serrated knife, put it to my wrist, and decided this was the day I would end my life. The deceit and excessive intoxication were beginning to wear down the little bit of life I had left, I thought. I would like to say it was because of the pain that I stopped, but it had to be because of God. I was hurting so badly internally, and all the warning signs were there, but no one was paying attention. Leroy had finally moved in, and my mom had completely changed into a different person. Those actions that I saw at my dad's house, with people whispering and moving as if they were invisible were now in our home. My mom put Leroy and us out almost every weekend, and as a result, we spent a lot of time with my brother. While I tried to confide in others, they were all in cahoots with her and knew the truth but didn't want to tell me. I thought it was only the alcohol but later find out she too was a crack addict. While I hoped this just began, I knew better.

Finally, my teacher noticed my cry for help and answered. When he first asked me to stay after class, I thought about what he could want. I wasn't stirring up any trouble, and my grade was an "A". Mr. Smith says to me, "Brandy, I know you are smarter than you put on. Why are you in this class." "I don't know", I replied. He says, "I'm going to get you moved to my advanced class because this is not where you belong." It was the first time in a long time that someone had thought about what was best for me. This improved my morale, and as I began to pay attention to class, I knew God had answered my prayers. Eventually, I met a friend, Myra. She and I hung out after school. It was nice to have someone to connect with, as I couldn't relate to any of the other girls at my school. Unfortunately, our friendship was short-lived. Anytime something was good, I was unable to be happy with it. The same girls with whom I had nothing in common now wanted to be friends. They were the ones who lived that black ghetto life that the movies so awfully portray. They cussed out adults, bullied people, and were not interested in school. I thought they were ok because they knew my cousin, but after some time, I saw that was all they knew. She tried to warn me, but I fell victim because she wasn't around as much anymore. I discarded my friend, who wanted to be somebody, for girls who wanted to show me I was no better than them. I regretted this when one day they asked me to fight my friend. She had done nothing to me, so what beef did I have with her. It was the requirement to fit in. This was a mistake on my behalf as she was almost three times my size and stronger.

I joined in as they bullied her, knowing this was not my character. It's funny because she was not fazed by any of it. She was probably more disappointed by my need for validation by people who only used me. One day on the school bus, it was decided that we would jump on her. I planned to initiate the fight and they would join in. This was not a well thought out plan. She would turn us, jumping her into her handling us all with no problem. The others jumped in, but if you asked me, I would say she won the fight that day. In turn, the bus driver took us back to school, and I was suspended from the bus for 10 days. How was I going to explain this to my mom? That was the last time I was ever in a clique. If I was going to be a pain in the rear, it was going to be for me. After this incident, I was ready for school to be over. There were only a couple of months until summer, and anticipation was building. In the meantime, my cousin and I found that the local recreation center had a double dutch team, and we joined. Although Myra and I would never be friends, I wouldn't be available to hang with that crowd again.

School was out and it was time I got into some real trouble. My mom worked during the day, so after my chores, I walked to my grandmother's, hoping to meet up with my cousins. Grandma was a no-nonsense type of woman. She was well known but kept to herself. I guess she figured she had enough children and grandchildren, and she had no time for anyone and their messy behavior. The good thing for me was that no one knew I was one of her grandchildren. Sadly, no one was ever happy to see you at my grandma's house. You would always be met with a look of *"why are you here?"* and the infamous *"where your mama?"*. No one really took much interest in my schooling or anything I was doing, but now I wonder if they knew how. There was so much animosity and jealousy among them as sisters and brothers that they could only focus on their own families. I never expressed how this made me look at my family. Thankfully, it wasn't like when I was dropped off, now that I was old enough to leave. So, I would go in and respectfully speak but kept it moving. My goal was only to make sure someone saw me if they were asked. Being there afforded me a life of freedom. It allowed me to step over the line without turning back. Although you had to tread lightly when you went into grandma's house, outside, you had free reign.

My grandma lived in the housing project "Dalton Village," and that's just what it was. It was a village of families that had lived here generationally since its inception and had planted roots from which each of them grew. Good or bad, everyone had their stories. I was always amazed when I visited the neighborhood because they had a foundation, something I knew nothing about. Because I was more like a visitor when I came through, I experienced more because no one knew my origin. This was in a time when a phone call was made if you were caught doing something you had no business. It was during the same time I searched for trouble. Typically, my mom would give me a few dollars and one day I decided to squander it. I already had a relationship with drinking but only flirted with smoking weed. In my brokenness, I was ready to change that.

Brooke and I were very close but due to her life being torn, she grew up quicker than she should. She was only two years only than me but carried herself like a grown up. Her friends were adults not little girls but the little girl inside her came out often. This was the time she was silly and acted like a normal teenager. Almost all my cousins dealt with life this way when our parents stopped parenting. We didn't want this life; this was what they forced down our throats.

When I arrived at my grandma's house no one my age was there. I sat around hoping someone stopped by and when Brooke walked through the door, I was happy. She wouldn't stay long, and I accompanied her when she left. Bored out of our mind, we decided to get high. She was headed to her dad's, and didn't have a lot of money, but I had enough for a dime bag. Foolishly, I emptied my pockets in order to buy the weed and Brooke bought the blunt. She grew up in Dalton Village and everyone knew her roots, so we had to find a place to hide out.

We went to her friend's house who was not home, but she had the key. She rolled the blunt and passed it to me to light but laughed when I barely inhaled. "What?" I asked, "what's so funny?". She replied, "You are not smoking. You didn't even inhale". We both broke out in laughter, and she said, "Here, let me show you". She began pulling on the blunt and then allowed the smoke to enter her lungs, let it marinate for a few seconds, and then exhaled. "Now you try," she said as she reached it for me. I was scared, but I wouldn't be lame, so I did exactly as she had instructed. As soon as I attempted to exhale, I started coughing. I thought something was wrong. "You alright, you alright," she said as she patted me on the back to keep me calm "Now you're smoking. Just let it marinate." I took a few more pulls before I began feeling different. We were laughing at everything and so hard. "You're high" she said, laughing.

Brooke told me earlier that she was catching the bus to her dad's, so after we finished the blunt, she walked me halfway back to grandma's house. It was Friday night, so I decided to stay and go home the next day. There was no way I could go home in this condition. When I arrived back at my grandma's house, she was fiddling in the kitchen, and my aunt sitting in the living room. I was the only kid at her house that night, so I sat with them. In an attempt to go unnoticed, I sat on the chair with the plastic on it or what was seen as the "forbidden furniture". This way, I could see everyone but be closest to the air conditioning as it was sweltering hot. My grandmother was upset and, in her fashion, was cussing up a storm, as they would say. I have never laughed so hard in my life. My aunt noticed my weird demeanor and whispered, "Are you high?" I couldn't lie, nor could I stop laughing. "Yes", I replied. "You better stop all that laughing before mama find out," she said, but I couldn't. Just then the phone rang, and it was Brooke. "Brandy, I need some bus fare. I got on the bus but forgot I didn't have any more money, so the driver told me to pay or get off. Can you bring it to me? I'm under the tree in the front hole," she said. "Ok" I replied, laughing about what happened the whole way. When I got there, it was extremely dark, and in her confused mind, she decided to stand under a huge tree. Why I will never know, but it just verified that she was just as high as I was. *We laugh about that moment even today.*

Being high became a go-to for me. Anytime I had some money, which wasn't often, I made my way to the Ville in hopes of running into Brooke. The thought never crossed my mind that I was an addict. I just thought I was smoking weed and at least I wasn't a crackhead. Oblivious to what it takes to be considered an addict, I enjoyed my addiction. A couple of weeks later, I ran into an old classmate, Toya. We met while at Wilson and became close friends but lost touch with the move. I was happy we reconnected. One day, she came over, and we walked to my grandma's house. During my visits, I became smitten with this boy named Thomas and found a reason to go around him when I could. Although we had been flirting for a while, he was looking for more of a loose girl, and I wasn't there yet. We attempted the girlfriend/boyfriend situation, but I was probably the only one in that relationship. I planned to go by my grandma's and hang out, hoping to run into him, but I wouldn't have to look far. We ran into him and his friend Joe as soon as we entered the neighborhood. We flirted for a while before they asked us to go back to Thomas's house. I knew what that meant, and since I was trying to appear grown, I was ready for it. I don't know what I expected for the first time, but it was the opposite. He put on some music, Scarface to be exact, and there was no warming up to it. When it was over, there was no warm kiss or hug. It was "ok", and we left. We talked about it on the walk back, and neither one of us understood why we had done what we had done.

When we got back, we were still high from our rendezvous. Although I don't understand why because nothing about it felt good, it just meant I was no longer a virgin. As I showed Toya the shed Sharon and I were cleaning out in hopes of throwing a party for my 14th birthday, Sharon stopped by. My mom had promised that I could have a party if I got it together, and I was motivated. I stopped cleaning so I could spill the tea. When I completed the story, she met me with a high five and the reply "OMG, you are a woman now cousin,". She was far from a virgin, but I wondered if she felt like this her first time, empty. It didn't matter. I played along, laughing, and clapping my hands, but honestly, I was rolling my eyes at what I had done. How had I given away the one thing that kept you sacred the key to becoming a "woman" at 13? However, it was years before I understood what becoming a woman truly meant, and it had nothing to do with sex. Nonetheless, I was eager to continue being seen as that "woman", by having more sex. This is why they say never say never. Here I was happy to be in another clique even though I denounced this months ago. My attitude, clothes, and walk changed into a fass little girl who thought she knew what she was doing. It wasn't long before I was at grandma's flirting with another guy. I liked him but he seemed out of my league, and now here, I was conversating with him. I don't have to tell you how it ended, but I will tell you I enjoyed every moment.

My birthday was near, and once again, I was met with the disappointment of my mom telling me I couldn't have a birthday party. After all that hard work I wanted to cry, but honestly, it was time I accepted the way it would be. Since it was the 4th of July anyway, I decided to hang out at my brother's house. He and Missy had reconciled, gotten engaged, and now lived across town. They had been through so much I hoped they could make it work this time. Sharon and I put on our cute outfits, scrounged up money, and headed by bus to their house. I wore my denim mini skirt, along with my white crop top and brown wedge sandals.

We arrived as the new girls on this side of town so of course we were being gawked. Once Ben let everyone know we were his little sister and cousin, it became more of a side eye. We hung out that day as Ben cooked on the grill. These times were few and far between, so I made sure I enjoyed the moment. We sipped and smoked, which made the day even more fun. No one questioned, and I was never denied the drink or the blunt. We couldn't go home because we were inebriated, so we decided to spend the night. The party continued well into my birthday, and we celebrated into the wee hours of the morning. Just as I was getting into my sleep good, I was awakened by Missy screaming and crying as she shook me to wake up. Startled and upset that she was waking me up, I sat up as she hugged me so tightly. She stated that she had a dream that I had been shot and killed. I was so tired that I wasn't absorbing much of her emotions but more concerned about how long she was going to keep me awake. Finally, she retired to her room, but not without breaking my sleep, so I flipped through the channels. I landed on a peculiar show that would never be anything that I would watch but was piquing my interest.

For us, having cable was a treat, but one thing that was forbidden was watching HBO after a certain time. It mostly consisted of shows that were for adults. Tonight, they were showing a documentary on crack cocaine. It showed real people as they did drugs and how and why they got into drugs. I did not understand why this was so interesting to me at the time. I knew a bunch of people who sold drugs, saw a lot of people buy drugs, but I never saw anyone do drugs. This saddened me as I thought about my dad and wondered how he was doing. After I shed a few tears and completed the show, I went back to sleep. As we woke up and went home, I decided to keep what I heard and saw to myself. Besides, I didn't want to relive any of it, nor did I want to continue feeling sorry for my dad. For the first time in a long time, I was happy to be home in my own bed. Before I took my shower, I went into my mom's room to get a towel from her closet. As I reached for the towel, a small bottle with aluminum foil dropped from the closet. WTF?!! The only thing I could think of was how long this had been going on and how my dad was so frowned upon when he wasn't the only one. I immediately went to my mom with the evidence, asking her what this was and why it was in her closet. It's possible she had either quickly learned to lie to herself, or she had been practicing what she would say, but the first and only answer she gave is that it was not hers. I thought, wait, someone got high and went into your room and hid this behind some stuff in your closet. "Ok," I replied.

Unfortunately for my mom, I was not done with this situation. We were already dealing with an absent parent, alcoholism from her and Leroy, and me having to raise my sister, and now this. They say when you look for something, you will find it, and I'm sorry, but I had become Sherlock Holmes to figure out what was happening in the place I called home. Is this why there was a certain stench in the house and so much whispering when certain people came by? Again, I asked questions, but no one wanted to be the snitch. Just as I was started to put down being a sleuth, I was in the bathroom cleaning when I stumbled upon what looked like the same crack pipe. Upset, I went to my mom once again only to be met with the same lies, "It's not mine. Someone must've put that there". They say that you cannot believe anything that someone on drugs says because they will lie to themselves just to get what they want. My mom was no different, and once I saw her reaction, I could identify each and every time she was lying. Since she had adopted this behavior of not worrying about what her decisions were doing to us, I decided I would follow suit.

The arguments between us became more and more intense as she was more concerned with partying rather than getting her life together. I couldn't take it anymore, so I took a break and went back to Ben's house. He was okay with me staying the weekend, but I was hoping it could be for much longer. Although I hated leaving Camila, it was different for her than for me. In a way, she was protected.

Although she probably witnessed more without me, that was not my concern. Quickly I was comfortable being at Ben's house. It was fun sitting on the porch with the music up, smoking and drinking. We always had sort of a non-official dance-off just to keep the good times rolling. As the night was just getting good, it was brought to my attention that I had a secret admirer. He had called my nephew over and asked my name. The next morning, walking across the parking lot, I heard someone call my name from a window. "Brandy," he said, "Who is that?" I replied, "Branndy," he said again. I replied, with my sassy tone, "If you're not going to show your face, don't call my name". That was just like me. Quick to reply, very slow to listen. Later that evening, while sitting outside again, he sent a message to ask me if I was in a relationship. "No, why?" I sent it back to him. He stated he wanted to get to know me, and his name was Daniel. Daniel, what type of name is that?

For days we sat in silence in company of one another only to spend hours at night on the phone. Eventually he asked me to be his girl-friend and I said yes. While he showed himself genuine, I knew that I was moving too fast. In the eyes of everyone else, this was cute, so I embraced the facade. In my mind, if it didn't work out so what I could move on to another one. The arrogance in my thinking was heightened the day I lost my virginity. That was the day I thought I knew what was best for me as I tried to run away from perils that masked itself as home.

Now that I was closer to Daniel, and school approached I begged my mom to let me go to West Meck. This meant I had to live with Ben, which was what I wanted, and I could keep an eye on Daniel. She said I could stay more of the summer, but she had to think about me living there. I even tried to persuade her by saying I wanted to attend my dad's Alma Mater. As it got closer to time for school, my mom continued to decline answering the question of could I stay and summoned me home. Because of her indecisiveness, I missed the first day of school and had to get my brother to intercede on my behalf.

She hardly listened to anyone except him, so he was always a card to pull if needed. He saved me yet again, and I was very grateful. So much happened that past year that I wanted to start on a clean slate. The negativity from my household was in my rearview. Now what were my goals? They say without a plan the people parish, but I thought I was beyond that thinking. It would not only hinder me but change my trajectory.

{ 5 }

LOVE?

The first day at high school high was like a reunion. It began with me getting registered and followed by reuniting with some old classmates and friends as I searched for my classes. I felt like a celebrity because I knew so many people. Although now I understand that God moves us to be in a better position, I was just happy to be back with my people. It was good to catch up and reminisce about the good times. I hoped to see Aaron, but found out that when he left Wilson, his mom switched him to a junior high that was a feeder school for West Charlotte instead. Instead of dwelling, I let the past be the past and focused on this new relationship. Part of my plan was already derailed when I found out Daniel lived with his grandma. He and I spoke when we could as he was never home. Although, I spent most of the time leaving messages, I found that this worked because I needed to find my purpose for wanting to be here. There needed to be something more than just being with Daniel and I needed to find it.

When he came home on Fridays, I was happy to see him bend the corner from the path. We spent as much time with one another since Missy was on me like a hawk. Someone had to because Ben would let me get away with anything since, he wasn't attentive to what I was doing. Two weeks into school, Daniel surprised me and transferred me to West Meck. Not that I wasn't happy that we saw each other every day, but I wasn't sure that Daniel was the one for me. It probably would have saved me a lot of worrying had I just been honest about that, but I wasn't. Instead, I went headfirst without knowing what to expect. Not that I wanted to be a floozy, but I wasn't sure I was ready for commitment. This had more to do with my newly found "woman hood" more than anything else. Besides I had yet to see a healthy relationship, so I didn't know how nor what it took. One thing I did know was if we were going to be in a relationship, we had to prove that.

Before long we were inseparable, but it was mostly after school. Because he wasn't well known, I was reluctant to be seen with him at school. Outside of homework and spending some time with Emily, he had the rest of my attention. My nose was wide open, and I couldn't care less about the consequences. Ben was usually asleep when I got home, and Missy had begun to work, so I had free reign until she came home. Before I moved with them, they seemed to be blissful but now there was an obvious disconnect. They were always off and on, so this was not unusual, but there was more to it. I didn't understand that Ben had a problem causing discord in their household. Although there was speculation, I had no proof that he was doing anything. It wasn't until I looked for a light and opened his matches that I understood I had jumped from the frying pan into the fire. He was doing drugs, too, and things were getting out of control. It was the first time I was disappointed with Ben. He was supposed to be saving me and he was the one needing saving. Knowing this information answered a lot of questions for me, such as why he and my mom were oddly close. They were walking similar paths and had become dependent on one another in order to make their delusional, crooked paths straight. Now, I was grateful that Missy was there to try to guide me because she didn't have to. She understood that without her, I would be completely lost.

Unfortunately, I couldn't see the forest for the trees and decided to hide my pain behind lots of sex and smoking weed. Thinking this way isn't helpful because while it took away my need for self-esteem, it allowed me to take support from people and things that meant me no good. I don't think Daniel started out to be that person, but he transformed very quickly. He was the only one I looked to for happiness, knowing I could trust him. We spent so much time together, but he was about to leash his true self onto me, and I was not ready for the fallout. Unbeknownst to me, Daniel had a girlfriend from his old neighborhood. I was appalled. This was why I had to leave a message for him to call me when he lived with his grandma. What surprised me the most was the fact he neglected to mention this to me. At that time, I didn't understand what a "red flag" meant but this was the perfect example. To top it off, I was at his house making out with him when she called. His sister was petty enough to let him know she was on the phone, and he was livid. Of course, he denied anything was happening and hung up the phone, but *69 was helpful, and I called her right back. Upset, I left with the broken promise of never being with him again. It was evident he wasn't a good guy, but when you have been betrayed and beaten down by the ones you trust the most, it doesn't matter. He shot me a few lies, and it was back to normal between us.

Just when I thought we had put this matter to bed, he thought he should befriend Adrian. Adrian was his brother's baby mama cousin whom Daniel foolishly said made them cousins. I knew him because we had gone to school together, and I knew that if Daniel wanted to be a better person, Adrian was not who he needed in his life. Although I voiced my opinion, Daniel decided to be his own man. Almost daily, Daniel went over to his house before coming home from school. Reluctantly, I sat back and watched as I could see the storm brewing. Emily and I were more focused on getting out of the hood at all costs, so we created a step team at school. While we didn't have a solid plan, we allowed our talents to take us as far as they could. Periodically, we stayed after school for practice, so today was not unusual. When I got home, I looked for Daniel, but he was nowhere to be found. This was weird as this was our usual time to see another. At first, I didn't think too much of it, but there was something in the pit of my stomach telling me something was off. So, I asked some of the people he hung with if they had seen him, but no one seemed to know anything.

I wanted to believe them, but I had this gut feeling someone was watching me. When his sister came outside, I asked, "Hey, where is your brother?", she looked at me with this look of I don't want to get in the middle of this and replied, "I don't know". I replied, "This isn't making sense how does no one know where he is". Daniel's family was very close. I have joked that they have a circle of trust, meaning they protect their own. So, for no one to know where he was made no sense, but it made sense that if they did, no one would talk. "Is he with Adrian?" I asked. "I don't know," she replied with a look that made me realize that she knew more than what she was stating. "All I know is he's in a house," she said. "Who's house?" I asked "Y'all's house?" She wouldn't respond, which only made things worse.

In the meantime, Emily walked up, and I told her what was going on. She attempted to keep my mind occupied, as she probably felt the same way I did, but she never expressed it. We continued with step practice as usual, but I kept looking over there for some reason. I could see in their door so if someone went passed it, I would know. Just then, I saw two people walking upstairs. Wait?! Everyone was outside, so who was that? I got up the courage to walk over to their house. I didn't want what was in my head to be true. His mom and dad were sitting on the porch. I spoke before I politely asked, "Is Daniel in there?", "yes," his father replied. I said, "Can you tell him to come outside?". "Daniel, Brandy wants you," his father would yell up the stairs. His father sat back down and said, "We don't have anything to do with this". Do with what? I questioned in my head. His parents were very progressive, so it wouldn't be a huge fuss if a girl was in there. What was everyone hiding from me other than knowing that Daniel was home all along? Shamingly, he came down. What was really happening at this point? I could tell from his demeanor something was off. "You have been here the whole time?" I asked, "No," he replied. I felt like he was lying. "What are you doing?" I asked "Nothing," he answered, "I just didn't feel like coming outside". What? We always were outside until dark so why didn't you feel like it today? I gave up on the conversation because I figured he was lying. I just needed to wait for the truth to be unveiled. We lived directly across from one another, so there was nowhere he could go that I wouldn't see him.

Getting impatient, I tried everything I could to get him to come back outside. I even called, but he was not biting. He kept telling me he was coming but never showed his face. At this point, I knew a girl was in there with him. Now, I just needed to know who this heifer was. There was no one that I saw him talking to that raised an answer of who it could be. If it was a female, how could he betray me when I had been nothing but good to him. Was this going to be the exchange I would have with everyone in my life? Was there going to be consistent hurt from everyone who stated, "I love you"? I couldn't answer these questions, but what I knew was if it was someone that when she came out, she was mine.

Just then, my phone rang. "Brandy, telephone", Missy hollered. This was before we could afford cell phones, so I had to go answer the phone. "Hello," I said "Hey Brandy this Brandy. The one who used to go with Aaron". WTF!! "Ok," I responded. "He doesn't know I'm calling you. I dialed *69 because I just wanted you to know I didn't know Daniel had a girlfriend, but nothing happened". Wait! So not only is this chick calling me from MY boyfriend's house, but I know this girl. I went to school with her and was never quite fond of her, but I had no real beef. She and Aaron were before my time, so I was curious to know why she thought telling me that was relevant to what was happening. It dawned on me; oh, she wants to be funny. I heard him say "Who are you talking to. You better not have called her". There were some other words right before the phone went dead. I called back, but no one answered.

I walked out the door and stormed across the parking lot like Sophia in The Color Purple. Missy and Emily constantly hollered my name, but I didn't want to hear anything. If he thought, he was going to disrespect me he had another thought coming. Again, I politely asked his parents to tell him to come outside, but neither she nor he came out the door. That's okay, I thought as I walked back toward the house. She had to come outside to go home. Just then, Missy called me into the house. What could she possibly want? Here I was in the middle of what seemed like a war, and she was distracting me because of a phone call. As soon as I walked through the door, she grabbed me while someone else shut and locked the door. What?! How was this happening? Apparently, Daniel had called, told her what happened, and asked her to please get me. I used every cuss word I could find and tried my best to get out. My boyfriend was caught red-handed, the chick called me to boast about it, they hid in the house, and as I was about to open a can of absolute rage, I got locked in the house. They were sadly mistaken because I would get to her no matter what. They allowed Emily to come in and attempt to calm me when, low and behold, her friend Tonya walked up the sidewalk. I told Emily, "Oh, she called her to try and jump me, ok". This only infuriated me more, and one thing was certain: I was going to get her. As they manned the front door, I opened the back door and ran around the house. Apparently, Emily snitched because I ran full speed, ready to fight anyone who stood in my way, when suddenly, I was yanked up like a freshly thrown newspaper on someone's lawn. I fought with everything I had to get loose, but it was no hope. I was manhandled back into the house by William, Missy's brother, and again locked down. I could not believe what was taking place. Suddenly, I saw them whisk her away like she was someone famous and I was her crazed stalker.

Once the storm calmed, I was allowed to go back outside. Feeling betrayed was an understatement of how I really felt. The people closest to me were probably protecting me from doing something stupid, but all I could see was betrayal. Emily went home as we all had school the next day. I decided I would sit in Ben's car as I wasn't quite ready to go in the house. While sitting there, a song that fit the situation came on. It was "Brokenhearted" by Brandy and Wanya. Just as the tears filled my eyes, Daniel's dad called me over. What could he possibly want? We met halfway in the parking lot, where he proceeded to tell me, "I know you're mad, but I will tell you what to do. You go to school tomorrow and find you a boy to eat lunch with. Y'all sit down, and you act like y'all are having a good time. That will get back at Daniel." What? I didn't want to get back at him. I wanted to slap his face and dump him in front of everyone for lying to me. I wanted to ring her neck for thinking she could attempt to make me look dumb. While we were talking, Daniel decided to walk up, but his dad motioned for him to go back. Were they trying to pull the wool over my eyes with this foolishness? I couldn't understand why his dad was "on my side". I took what he said with a grain of salt and went about my way. Daniel later found the strength to walk over and provide half an excuse and apology. He stated she just showed up and wouldn't leave. He knew he couldn't be seen with her, so he told her to come in so I wouldn't find out. Nothing he said changed how I felt. He stated none of this would've happened had I acted like we were in a relationship at school. Huh?! How did this turn on me? Ok, so let's change that and see. I was big on testing theories to prove my point. The next day, he walked me to class. His good graces wouldn't last but a hot minute before it was some more mess.

Now that he was Adrian's sidekick, more people learned who he was. He spent more time at Adrian's house and less with me. A part of me felt he was going there to meet up with someone. Possibly Brandy. Even though this bothered me, I found ways to stay busy. Although I tried to convince myself otherwise, everything was about him, and he knew this. This probably ushered in the endless amount of disrespect I was due to receive, but I stayed. I turned into exactly what I despised. Someone who does whatever it takes to be with a guy. I saw this repeatedly at this time in my life and vowed that this would never be me. Unfortunately, I went down the same path at 1000 mph. I wouldn't admit why at the time, but while the right people didn't love me, I had forgotten how to love myself. People seem to think depression comes with crying and sitting in a lonely room, but it doesn't. I was able to be around people every part of every day, yet I never felt so lonely. I was surrounded by individuals who only thought of themselves, but I kept a smile and cried myself to sleep most nights. I got so good at it; I thought I was happy.

Things changed slightly when Daniel started working and giving me anything I asked for. Sad to say but it was never enough to fill the hole inside of me. He probably tried to be a good guy, but I couldn't accept it. He had betrayed our bond, so although I accepted everything, it meant nothing. Instead of appreciating, I desecrated everything. Ben and Missy fought as their happiness had become unraveled, and I could feel a shift in the atmosphere. The change she hoped for during their separation was short lived. His habit had taken over once again, and they were at risk for losing the apartment. Amid it all, my father re-surfaced. The last time I saw or heard from him was over a year ago. He was supposed to be in Winston-Salem getting well but from the looks of nothing had changed. While it was a surprise, it was the good news I needed. Although he looked a mess, I was happy to see him. We spent the next few days together, visiting thrift stores and enjoying one another's company. He asked about what I had been up to and talked about getting himself together, to which I believed him. As they say, all good things must come to an end, and they did. As we sat on the porch, he noticed something going on with my neck. Usually, I wore a scarf around my neck to hide it, but it was too late. Daniel had lined my neck with hickeys, and it was then my father asserted his parental rights. I know what you're thinking, but back then, they were the thing to have. At least that's what I thought. He quickly equated them to sex, and it was over. Now I can say while we were sexually active, but these were not sexually provoked. According to my dad, I was on the path to pregnancy, and I must be stopped. He called my mom and that was all she wrote. She told me to pack my bags, and it was back home. I could have spit fire I was so mad at my dad. How dare he come back after all these years of being an absent parent and uproot my happiness? I called Ben and begged him to talk to mom. It worked, but there were restrictions. I had to come home every weekend and on holidays. I despised this but suffered silently.

As quickly as he had come, my dad was gone again. He was a little closer, but I saw him no more than when I didn't know where he was. He moved into a boarding house with his girlfriend and promised he would do better. His actions and the way he moved so quickly; I knew that was a lie. Old habits die hard, and I later found out he was only there because he was running from someone. However, he did find the time to call, so we gave him credit. Some weekends, my mom sent Camila to spend the weekends at Ben's, too. These were some of the times we actually got along, as I had nowhere to go but in the parking lot with Daniel. Besides, she had our niece to hang out with, so it worked. During one of her visits, my dad stopped by, which was very unusual but not unwanted. He asked my sister and I what we wanted for Christmas. We were excited as Santa Claus hadn't visited nor been mentioned in our house for so long. We usually just waited to see what gifts my mom had gotten from the Christmas Bureau and griped about it not being what we asked for. She always had some clever excuse as to why we didn't get what we wanted, so I just stopped asking; it was easier. Besides, we could tell she didn't have any emotion because she wouldn't spend the $2 for wrapping paper. She just left them in the black plastic trash bags they came in. We both asked for some Reebok Classics, as they were in style at the time. He promised us we would have them; we had no reason to doubt it.

On Christmas morning, we were thrilled about getting our new shoes. After we watched my niece and nephew enjoy their new toys, we decided it was time to put those smiles on our faces. It was very cold as it had snowed and iced a few days earlier. We made sure to put on our starter jackets that we received two years ago from my aunt and her boyfriend. We talked along the 15–20-minute walk about the outfit we would wear with our shoes. We arrived ever so happy to see our dad but happier to get some new shoes. He invited us in out of the cold but walked us into a blizzard. As he opened the door, I was surprised to see that Norma was back. Clearly, we interrupted things, so we decided to get our gift and go. Drugs and alcohol weren't the only things that separated us from our parents, we had Leroy and Norma to thank for that as well. Neither one of them were perfect stepparents with Norma being the worst. Today was too good to allow her nasty attitude to mess it up. We ripped through the gift wrap, and there they were, our first pair of real named brand shoes. It wasn't but a second before those smiles were turned upside down. The shoes were the wrong size and not the style we had asked for. He promised to take and exchange them, so we left empty-handed and headed back to Bens. I knew we needed to go that day because if we left, he wasn't going to take them back. Unfortunately, I had to be optimistic for Camila because she was just getting to know him, and I was all she had to look up to. That was the last we saw of him and those shoes for years to come.

Being let down was hard enough, but now that Camila was getting older, it heaped more on my shoulders. I was tasked with talking her down from whatever antic she decided to get into. Now that I came home on the weekends, she and I were able to talk, and I told her I was trying to get out of here. While there my mom complained about how out of control Camila had become. She had threatened teachers and been kicked out of school. What my mom didn't want to face was she helped create this personality she possessed.

As time passed, we did our best to put away our emotions about dad so we could continue living. He'd made it clear through his actions, that we were not his primary focus. Because we both wore our emotions on our sleeve, it was hard to say who hid it best. As summer approached, I prepared to move back home. This was part of my punishment so there was no need to be upset. Although I was reluctant to go, it was comforting to be back in my own bed for a while. Since they only had two bedrooms at Ben's my unofficial room was the living room. It was hardly convenient, but I made it work. While at home she'd made it clear I wasn't to go to Ben's, but it didn't stop me from sneaking over. This was the reaction from her finding out I was sexually active and placing me on birth control during spring break. Instead of her explaining the importance of STD's she was more focused on me getting pregnant. This led to me thinking more about one than the other and stopped using protection other than birth control. While she was focused on me getting to Daniel, she neglected to see the harm of me being at home.

Men were so used to getting what they wanted off this street, but it surprised me when I was a target. I wasn't overly built with a big butt and breasts. I mean, you could tell I was a child. Not that it excused their actions if I weren't. Obviously, predators don't care when they want what they want. While walking across the street to the store, I stopped to call Daniel, which was nothing unusual. My mom and aunts were sitting in the front yard, so I wasn't too uncomfortable; besides, it was broad daylight. While on the phone, I noticed a Caucasian man behind me in a van. At first, he asked me from the van, but I couldn't hear what he said. I told Daniel what was happening. He said, "What is he talking to you for?" "I don't know," I replied. We continued talking on the phone, and I turned my back hoping to show him that I was uninterested. Whatever his motives were, he was focused. When I got off the phone, he called me over again. Thoughtlessly, I went, and to this day, I cannot understand why. As I approached, he asked, "Do you want to make some money?" "No," I replied. "You don't have to do anything," he followed up. "No," I replied. Just as I was walking away, he said, "All you have to do is talk to me on the phone for 5 minutes". I stopped in my tracks and turned around to ask, "How much?". "$20" he proposed. "No," I replied. "$40," he said. Reluctantly, I said, "Ok," knowing what I was doing was wrong on so many levels. I justified it by saying technically I wasn't doing anything wrong, and I heard girls do a lot more for less. Truthfully, I was 14, broke, and wanted the money to make phone calls or catch the bus, I shouldn't have said yes, but I did.

At first, the conversation was "innocent," with him only asking me questions about me to which I answered none of them. Suddenly, the conversation took a turn, and I realized this was not a game. Although I tried playing hard, I was terrified that this man would do something to me. I told myself not to show any weakness. He asked me over and over if I would pull up my shorts a little and I declined. Even offering more money if I did yet I still declined. I was distraught enough with what I was doing so the audacity to ask for more wasn't going to happen. Besides how bold did you have to be to ask for this sort of thing in broad daylight and not worry about being caught. He kept his word, and in five minutes, I was done and relieved. After he reached me my money, I went home and told my mom exactly what happened. I expected her to lash out and tell me how wrong it was or hug me while thanking God this man didn't take me. Maybe look for the guy or call the police, but she didn't. She explained what happened, while someone else asked did I at least get paid. When I answered "yes" it was as if this wasn't as bad as I was making it out to be. Ugh! This made me more aware and when it looked like this was going to happen again, I took charge.

That same summer, as I walked to my grandmother's house, a car containing an older Caucasian gentleman drove past. As he drove downed the street and noticed me, he slowed down to get a good look. This put a serious fear in my heart. It was midday, so traffic was not heavy at all. If something were to happen to me, no one would know because no one knew I was gone. After he passed by, I saw him turn around only to slowly drive past me again. My first instinct was to tell him off, but I ran instead. There was still about 2 miles to go to get to my grandmother's house, but I wouldn't stop until I reached her door. You could have called me Forrest Gump that day because "I WAS RUN-NING". When I arrived, she first asked why I was running. I don't remember many conversations between us, but I was glad to have this one with her. She assured me that I did the right thing. Afterwards I decided to get on the bus rather than walk to her house alone.

I cannot explain how this situation and so much more would shake up my thoughts about men. I had no trust in them. Every one of them I had met until this stage of my life was full of nothing. Lying, conniving, distrustful men who deserved no place in my life. These thoughts spilled into my adult life in ways you cannot imagine. Especially since a lot of the men who made me distrust their species were men whom I looked to respectfully. As I sit here and remember that moment, I wonder how many times those men have tried other girls my age. Also, how many of them were able to leave unscathed? It's scary to think and even scarier to learn the answer. Unfortunately, this made me use their arrogance towards women to get what I wanted, and I felt no shame. Sometimes, it worked out for my good, but sometimes they expected more than I was wanted to give.

Once again, we moved, but it was back to the blue house in Lakeview. This time, it was the front apartment, which was bigger, but it was back to the one bedroom. Although we had only been gone just shy of two years, we had all changed significantly. I was embarrassed to be back, but I had no choice. My brother's drug habit worsened, and they had to move in with Missy's brother. Apparently so did my mom's even though we were told the reason for the move was the landlord wanted to sell the house. He and my mom were off the Richter Scales, and their loved ones had to endure the blowback. There was an upside to this with me being closer to Daniel and not having to switch schools. I too had developed a drug habit, weed and alcohol, and since I was in walking distance, walked to Daniels frequently to drink or smoke. Daniel's parents were nontraditional, so some of the things I wouldn't dare to do with my mom were able to be done at their house. The boys were treated more like adults even though he was only two years older than me. I graduated to spending the night just because I could. My mom was furious not just about the audacity of me but why his parents allowed this. As a result, she continuously called the police who politely escorted me home. She knew where I was, so I didn't understand the need for the police. Trying to deter her was impossible so I told Daniel to get us a hotel room. Since his brother was not home, he got one of the neighborhood guys to get it for us. That didn't last long as she sniffed me out. My brother knew the guy who got us the room, so it didn't take much for him to rat us out. After tiring efforts, she sent me to live with Ben for the rest of the summer. This only enraged me more because I felt like she was throwing me away. Ben no longer had a home and the people he lived with were very disapproving. When I wanted a mom, she needed me to grow up and now that I was being grown, she pretended to parent. This was very confusing to say the least. Instead, of her having the conversation with me, she thought these people who judged everyone were better for me. It didn't matter because I intended to run away from them too.

Just like the predators before, he could tell I was a girl who was broken. That's how he was able to swoop in and try to break me more. So, when we we're introduced, I could see his intentions clearly while my hope was to use him. At least this was what I was told I should do to him. I guess this was part of my "becoming a woman, " and I foolishly went along with it. His name was Bryan, and he was 10 years older than I. As I look back, he was what I would call a clown now, but then he was a cornball with money. Since they wouldn't allow me to see Daniel, I called Bryan. My brother knew nothing, but I told his girlfriend where I was going, and she said nothing to the contrary. I'd met with him before to smoke, and nothing happened, so I wasn't concerned about leaving with him again. What I didn't know was he only allowed me to think I was in control so he could earn my trust. That afternoon he took me to the mall, and afterwards, we went to a motel room. Now never in my memories do I ever remember telling him this was where I agreed to go. He lied to me and said he had to stop here for a minute. That was fine until he convinced me to come in which made me nervous. This was planned because he already had the key. After I asked him to take me home several times, I called my brother's girlfriend. I was not going to have sex with him. I was still in a relationship with Daniel and besides I didn't like him that way. Although I tried to be strong, I was terrified. He said, "If you just do what we came to do, then I will take you home". Do what we came to do? When did I consent to going to a hotel with you to "do" anything? It wasn't until she threatened to send the police to the room that he took me home. That was the last time he and I spoke, or I tried that foolishness. I never told anyone what happened. I just let it be a lesson learned.

It affected me in ways I couldn't imagine.

Interlude

i gave birth to you prematurely,
the labor was endless, i thought you could save us, mend what was broken and bridge the gap between mind and speech, but each and every step you took only increased the distance, therefore, I christened you Silence. I heeded your cries, swaddled you in blankets, and rocked your crib for ages.
                    i thought you could save us

                              ~Davion Alexander

{ 6 }

Damage

As it got closer to the first day of school, I was allowed to come home. The old neighborhood was the same but different. Not in the sense of appearance, but everyone had gone from innocent lives to everyone who wanted to be an adult. I was high almost every day, and now I was smoking cigarettes, too. Now that we were closer to Daniel, I caught the bus to his house, hung out, and walked home. By this time, I had given up on my dreams. Now, I was just trying to fit in anywhere I could. Whether it was doing what everyone else was doing or attempting to be who I thought I needed to be, I was no longer the Brandy destined for greatness.

My mom worked my teenage nerve, and her habits had gotten worse. Most times, I was home alone, and I cannot remember a school day when I came home to my mom making dinner. We no longer had a home. It was four walls that wreaked of a stench that would never go away, no matter how much I cleaned. So much so that I spent the night at Daniel's on the weekend. Money was being stolen, lies were being told, and now she was coping right before my eyes. She thought it was cute to wave at me as she knocked on the dope man's door while I was sitting with my friends. Not only that but he was a friend of mine. Even though it was no secret to everyone, I didn't want to see it. I was embarrassed and enraged beyond words.

No one understood how angry I was because I always kept a smile on my face. The problem with not expressing my feelings meant that somehow these emotions would erupt. Unfortunately, it wasn't long before I couldn't contain what I was feeling. There was a girl who I was told was interested in Daniel. She was younger and timid, so me approaching her probably would have been enough. Unfortunately, I needed to make someone feel even worse than myself. One afternoon I caught the school bus to Daniel's house to spend time with him, and right before I left was told she was walking toward the store. This is where you have to be careful who you call your friends because the people who told me where she was were her friends. I approached her and accused her of something she was adamantly trying to convince me was a lie. As she turned around to walk away, I felt disrespected and, in true bully fashion, grabbed her by the back of her hair, yanked her to the ground, and slammed her head into the concrete. This was right before I threatened her to stay away from Daniel or I was coming back. As I walked home, I was disappointed in myself. I had no right to do this to her, nor was it warranted. It hurt to find out that when Missy heard what happened, she talked about me like a dog. Like I had never saw her go ape about my brother. What she didn't expect was Daniel to correct her and request she say that to my face. He knew what I was dealing with and was sure to let them know they were doing nothing to help remedy the problem.

Maybe that was the part that kept us bound to one another: loyalty. Or maybe it was the trauma that he and I experienced in our childhood. Either way, now, we were ten toes down for one another. Or so people thought. As the old saying goes, you never know what goes on behind closed doors. We didn't trust one another, and he was always linked to some girl, and I had a crush on a guy named Luther. After the incident with Brandy and the other girl, I was hopeful there was no one else. But for some reason, there was ALWAYS someone he was interested in, including me, and I hated it. It was bad enough dealing with my own past killing my self-esteem, and now this guy I cared about was making it worse. There were rumors that he desired another young lady in the neighborhood. All I could think was here we go again. So back over there I went, ready to confront yet another girl. I cannot remember our argument that day, but I took his bookbag with some "valuable" things inside and placed it on the back porch while he was on the front. When he came back inside, this was the first thing he noticed. This enraged him. I guess I could've told him where it was, but again, I was a rebel. This led to something I would never have expected. Before I could think about what was coming, he grabbed me by the throat and choked me until I passed out. When I came to, I was so afraid and so hurt. All of this because I put your bookbag on the back porch? I left crying my eyes out. I saw the girl he was accused of messing around with, and she asked me what was wrong. I replied, "You can have him. I'm done". While I walked home, I was tried to understand what was wrong with me. Why were all the males in my life sucking at what they were put on this earth to do, protect? Better yet why I allowed them to?

When I reached the railroad track that led to my home, I heard someone call my name. I turned around, and there he was, standing like some guy in a romantic movie. It was like a scene right out of the movie "The Notebook". He wiped the tears from my eyes and grabbed my hands. Just like that, I accepted his apology and went back to him. I felt so dumb. How could I allow this boy to raise a hand to me? How could I not slap him for what he did to me and keep walking? I wanted very much to end everything about our relationship. The issue was that at this time in my life, I needed someone who loved me, and it was Daniel. The problem with my thinking was that this was not love. You don't do this to someone you care about. Wouldn't you guess, internally I blamed myself and thought I could fix him. So, I came up with a plan to fix him without him knowing. I forgave him and blamed the girls for his actions. If given the opportunity, I would apologize to them. I knew I wasn't happy with him then, but I wasn't happy with me either. I was dead inside.

The emotional rollercoaster I was on was nauseating. The concept of love had no place in the life I lived. Slowly Luther and I developed a friendship. At first, it was a big brother type deal as he was in the 12th grade, but it grew. For me, anyway. It felt nice conversing with someone who had no ties so no obligations were expressed. Although Luther showed himself as an obvious choice, Daniel was still in my life, so I tread lightly. It didn't stop me from getting excited to see him in our Economics class. He asked if he could come pick me up and hang out, and I obliged. I asked my cousin to ride with us to make sure things were casual. It was nice to ride out, laugh, talk, and of course smoke with no intentions behind things. Unfortunately, our friendship was short-lived when he graduated in January, and we lost touch. A few years later, I found out he was killed as I browsed through the newspaper. What's sad is that I couldn't mourn my friend for fear of what it would look like.

Mr. Davis, my Economics teacher, opened my eyes to a brighter future. He and my father were classmates, and he took a special interest in giving me a better life. We discussed the prospect of me going to college. In the beginning I was excited about going to college but every day that passed that dream faded. Instead, I figured I should get pregnant. It was as if my life wasn't low enough that I needed to bring an innocent child into it. But I figured that this baby would fill the hole where love should have been. This was very selfish of me as there was no one else I thought of before I made the decision. Valentine's Day, 1997, Daniel and I visited the Knights Inn motel. I was no longer taking birth control, so I knew what could happen that night. On the walk home the next morning, I knew I was pregnant. There was a feeling inside of me. Keeping this thought to myself was easy. No one paid that much attention to how I felt to question if I was going through anything.

After I missed my period, I made my own appointment at the clinic. I told my cousin, Kenya, I had an appointment, and she agreed to accompany me. Emily's sister drove our school bus and did us a favor by dropping us off. Funds were limited, so I appreciated her help. I think Kenya was more nervous than I was because I knew I was pregnant. I intentionally made this happen, but I played along. When the doctor came in with the results, she was probably more nervous than I should have been. "You're pregnant," Dr. Smith said reluctantly. Afterwards, she gave me a heartfelt speech and asked me a question I hadn't considered in all my arrogance. "Are you going to be ok with telling your mom?" she asked. Honestly, I hadn't considered telling her, so my answer to that was "Ummm no". I may have been bold enough to do this, but I wasn't bold enough to tell my mom. She said, "call and set up an appointment, and we can all discuss options". Afraid of what Kenya would think, I walked out of the room and signaled to her I would tell her what happened when we left. That was just before the doctor opened her mouth with, "Don't forget to make your appointment". "Why does she want to see you?" Kenya asked to which I mumbled, "I'll tell you in the elevator". After telling her my truth, she did nothing but embrace me and tell me she was with me no matter what my decision was. I knew what my decision was, but I pretended that abortion was an option.

A few days later, we received a call from the clinic. My mom reacted to the voicemail the doctor left. It said, "Ms. Anderson, this the doctor from the clinic, and I would like to make an appointment to speak with you concerning Brandy. If you would please return my call." She stood in the living room as I came through the door and asked, "Why is the clinic calling me about you?" What excuse was I going to use? "I don't know", it was the one excuse I had used time and time again. "Don't lie to me," she demanded. I waited a few moments trying to find the right lie to tell her, but nothing came to mind. "Brandy!" she exclaimed. "Yes," I replied. "Why does this doctor want to speak with me concerning you?" My voice got very low at this point, and I cowardly replied, "I'm pregnant." My mom was livid. "Pregnant!" she yelled. "What in the world are you thinking. You are too young to have a baby. Besides, you are messing up your future. You are going to have an abortion". My mom was a teenage mom and bride. If I were me now, I could see myself telling my 15-year-old the same thing. A child has no place to be a mom, but because I was so damaged inside, there was only one response I had, "No". How was the woman who had not mothered me in years going to stand in front of me and tell me to get rid of my baby? I was so ready to be done with her that I wasn't about to mess up my plan. After she finished her motherly speech, I left to call Daniel. I couldn't call him from home because she was upset, so I walked to the phone booth. I told him as soon as I found out, but he hadn't told his mom yet either. After telling him what happened with my mom I asked if he was going to tell his mom. Although she wasn't as brass as my mom, I could tell she wasn't happy about our decision either. Selfishly, I couldn't care less what anyone thought. This was my baby, and I was unwavering on whether it would make it to this world or not.

The pregnancy itself was a breeze. No morning sickness or heavy weight gain, and Daniel and I were as thick as thieves, or so I thought. My mom attended the first doctor's appointment with me only to find out she made an appointment with a pediatrician and not an obstetrician. It wasn't her fault, that's who Medicaid assigned me to, and we both laughed at his reaction when he saw me. These were the days I longed for. Since it was late in the school year, my mom allowed me to stay at West Mecklenburg. Although I was happy in private, I was ashamed in public. Once I began to show, I wore a jacket. It was hard for me to understand I was giving up my childhood. Honestly, I hadn't known what that was since the day we left Todd's Park, but I was hopeful. If only I could have understood how much I was changing my life, I would never have made this decision. What was even more dissatisfying was when I got home and hid myself from judgment. Although I wasn't the first teenage mom, it was like I was being scrutinized. Maybe it was because they saw more from me, and I had disappointed them. Nonetheless, it would've been nice to have someone say, "I know what you're going through, and I'm here if you need me". Towards the end of the school year, my mom told me to say good-bye, and she changed my school. Inside, I felt like I was isolated from my world, but I understood her logic. THIS was now my world. So, I said my goodbyes to good ol' high school and looked forward to TAPP (Teenage Pregnancy and Parenting Program) the next school year.

Because of my appointments, I missed too many days and was subjected to summer school. It was the only thing keeping me home during the week. However, on the weekends, I spent time at Daniel's. In my mind, I figured what else could happen I was already pregnant. Besides, my mom and I were still at odds, so I tried to stay away as much as possible to keep some peace. It became a challenge when Daniel started tryouts and workouts for football. Incidentally this was the exact time one of the men from my neighborhood thought we should be friends. While I wondered what changed about me to warrant this friendship, I entertained the conversation anyway. Although his motives were probably something different, I wasn't interested. He was almost twice my age and thought he could buy my affection. He was helpful when I had to pull on him for money to pay our phone bill. Although he said if I needed anything to ask, I was careful not to send the wrong message, so I made that the first and last time. As long as I wasn't with Daniel, my mom wasn't too concerned about me being elsewhere. Besides, I was already catching the evil eye from his ex-girlfriend, who used to be an associate of mine when we smoked. We were cool so I wouldn't cross that line. Some would probably say why do that and I tell those people that you will never understand until you have understood what was like to be me.

My mom continued to embarrass me when she could. Most times I just took it because reacting only made it worse, but I stood up for something this summer. Two weeks before my 16th birthday, she came home to me finger-waving my neighbor Julie's hair. This was nothing new; I would do hair to make a little hustle, and she never said anything. I knew she was drunk when she stumbled through the door. She asked, "What the hell ya'll doing in here? Ya'll need to take that shit somewhere else." "Ok, ma. I'm almost done," I replied. She wasn't letting up, so I told Julie we could just finish at her house. Besides, she started with Julie, and Julie replied with impolite responses. One thing I was not going to allow to happen was for someone else to think it was ok to disrespect my mom.

As I packed things up to leave, my mom jumped on my back, "you're not going anywhere," she said as we fell into the chair. Julie and I were able to get her off me, so I went to her house to call Daniel. He instructed me to call a cab, but when the cab arrived, she had left the house. As I was getting in on one side, she was getting in on the other. "What are you doing?" I asked. While we went back and forth about her not going anywhere, the cab driver insisted we decide because he had to go. Just then, Daniel, his dad, and the police pulled up at the same time. Daniel jumped out to make sure I was ok. The police! Who called them? Before I could answer, she walked towards the police while she attempted crocodile tears, as she accused me of hitting her. Really?! I was seriously being questioned by the police on allegations that I had done something that I thought about but would never do. The entire street was filled with people watching the spectacle on their porches. Laticia was the only one to get involved by coming to my defense and telling the police that this was a lie, and my mom was forever showing out on me. The police were apologetic about what I was going through and, instead of locking me up, gave me some nuggets. "When will you be 16?" he asked. "In two weeks," I replied. "Well, that's good. If you can hang in there two more weeks, you can leave, and she cannot call the police to come get you." This was the best news I heard all day. At the same time, my aunt pulled up. The police explained to her what happened, and she convinced them I was ok in her care. Daniel stayed behind to protect me. He didn't say much but I could tell he wanted to vanquish my mom. Once my aunt had my mom distracted by whatever, she told us to get in the car and duck down. She dropped us off at Daniel's house, and I stayed off and on there for the duration of the summer.

When it was time for school, I decided to go home. My mom and I spoke, and she promised things would get better, but I knew they wouldn't. TAPP's was very different from traditional high school. The goal here was to help you navigate the difficulties of being a teenage parent while providing you with the resources to complete your education. It benefited girls in my position, but I felt more out of place than I had in my entire life. Here I was with girls whose story was probably more like my own, yet we couldn't be any more different to me. Not that I thought any less of them, just more of me, so much so that I decided I wouldn't make any friends. During registration, they'd made me aware that I had completed most of my credits in high school, and If I stayed focused, I could have my baby and graduate a year early. The school even had a nursery, so I didn't need to worry after I had him. We both could go to school, and I could graduate. The possibilities for myself had not ended, but I needed to work hard.

My weeks consisted of focusing on graduating, so the more I stayed home the better. Daniel made the football team, so I attempted to make each home game. I tried to get to away games, but it was a little harder. Most times, I had to ask Leroy's friends and family for a ride or money to catch a cab. Most kidded that I was very resourceful, but they couldn't imagine the amount of repulsion I had to have to ask these men for money. It was the only way because my mom was hell-bent on not giving me money and neither was Daniel. She knew I wasn't coming back until Sunday or Monday after school, and there was nothing, she could do about it. By this time, my belly was in full swing. I could hear the whispers at the games as I cheered him on. Some were from girls who were trying to be with him, and others were concerned parents who wanted to know why my mom allowed me to get pregnant. I tried my best to ignore it all as I cheered him on. His coach told him college was an option, so he was working hard to make that a reality. It was clear that his eyes were focused on his future. I could see it as we watched his highlights from the game when they were featured on the news. I couldn't blame him because I never considered what he wanted at the time I came up with my plan. For that matter, I didn't think about what I really wanted. Where I should have focused on my future, I gave that up because things weren't going right in the present. He wasn't showing any rebuttal about anything, so I just assumed he was ok with everything. I'm sure the talk about me from his family was unflattering downstairs when I stayed the weekend, but I was willing to suffer it just to be with him. Although they smiled, you could see they weren't thrilled about me being there and I felt the tension. It was ok because I was ready to take care of my child on my own, or so I thought.

As the football season was ending, my mom decided to move. I came home to wash and get clean clothes, only to find out they were on the way out. My mom had not told me anything about moving. She was well within her right since I was always over Daniel's house. Also, I had demeaned her position as my mom with my actions. The new place was across town; while it was not a mansion, my sister and I finally had separate rooms. This was convenient since the baby was coming soon. Although I was sad to be further away from Daniel, I was happy to get out of Lakeview. Nothing, and I mean nothing good, had come of us moving there. My hope was this move allowed us to get our mom back. I knew her potential and hoped being here would be the push she needed to improve. It was a three-bedroom, one bath brick house on a dead-end street. While it too was what they would call a "shot gun house" I was happy to be here. My room was next to the kitchen, connected by a door that proved useful. It made it easier to make the bottles late at night. We had a nice sized backyard leading to a creek separating us from the highway. The highway was very noisy until they put up the noise protectors. Unfortunately, our front yard became the gathering place for drinking once again. It wasn't until a family friend announced that the dope house was two houses up that people's ears perked up and I knew we were still in a bad situation.

As my due date approached, I was nervous and worried about what would happen. School was going well, and I was finally settling in. I had begun my senior exit and was on track to graduate. My problem was that I was more focused on November 19th, which was my due date. Just like everything else in my life, I felt like it had to happen when they said it would. I promised myself that if I didn't, I wouldn't go back to school. None of that remotely made any sense, but it seemed like nothing I did ever make any sense. Especially now. In true first-time baby fashion, the baby did not come on time, so I held up my end of the bargain. I left school that Friday and didn't return. The doctors told me that if I didn't go into labor in a week, then I would be induced. So, against my better judgment, I moved to Daniel's house. What I couldn't and still don't understand is why I was so drawn to this man instead of living for myself. I put myself in situations that I didn't have to be in, trying to make something from nothing. His family didn't like me, but they tolerated me, and I could feel it. People don't understand that you will do anything not to feel that way again when you're abandoned or felt abandoned. Here, I was living in a place that in no way felt like home, with a person who was in no way my home. My vision of home is a place filled with love, peace, strength, growth, God, all things that relate to a positive upbringing. To top that, I was about to bring a child into this misery in hopes of changing the way I felt about myself. After trying everything, and I mean everything, I went into labor. I was afraid but happy at the same time. Although it happened in the middle of the night, Daniel was able to get his mom to take us to the hospital. I called my mom, but she came later the next day. She brought with her my aunt, and they were both drunk and probably high, if I had to guess. For as long as it took her to show, it only took minutes before she was gone again. I understood she didn't agree with my decisions, but I couldn't understand how she could leave me. This was the second-class behavior she exhibited towards me since their separation that I promised never to do to my children. After 29 hours, we welcomed our son and named him D.

Before we moved, I had and unofficial baby shower. There wasn't a big party, but I was blessed with some items that would present themselves useful once the baby arrived. Laticia gave me all her son's clothes who was born earlier that year, and my mom gave me a vintage baby bed. This was one of those moments she proved that she loved me that I hoped lasted longer than it did. When I had money, I too bought things, so I didn't need much in the beginning. Because I was indigent, I received assistance through Medicaid, WIC, and Child-care Resources which were all needed. God had made a way for me to do this on my own if I needed to. It wasn't what I wanted, though, I wanted to be surrounded by as much family as possible.

The day I came home with the D, it was not filled with roses as I had hoped. Camila was excited, but my mom had a look of I don't know how to feel on her face. I pretended to be ok, but I wasn't. Where was everyone? No one from Daniel's side of the family, not even Daniel, was there to meet us. There was no real support from them, especially since his sister was pregnant at the same time. Instead of worrying about what wasn't, I should've been focusing on being a mom. D had been in the nursery at the hospital, so I had no idea what his habits were overnight. Besides that, the only example I had of being a parent was from babysitting. The difference was that they went home, so I was unprepared for this journey. My mom tried to tell me to rest but I was doing things my way once again. I socialized as much as I could, although no one truly had any interest in sitting and talking with me. A few words were exchanged as they passed through, going outside or to the bathroom. My only concern was that he was warm, as we were not allowed to cut the heat on until after five. You can deduce what that meant. From watching movies, I was delusional about bringing babies home from the hospital. I thought I would bathe and feed him, lay him in his bed and all would be right with the world. Just as my brain entered its REM cycle, I heard a noise that surpassed any I had ever heard. D was hollering, or should I say screaming, and for what, I had no idea. I tried everything with fail before we were both crying, and I was screaming for my mom. I begged my mom to please get him, and she obliged after telling me she told me. Reality had set in, and I had no business being a teenage parent.

From the moment D was born, I could tell Daniel was not ready to be a parent. Not that I didn't see that prior, but it was like a slap in the face that I was not going to have the happily ever after I was hoping for. I cannot say he didn't love his son, but I did know he didn't love this situation. I cannot remember him coming to see about us once we came home, which bothered me. He was concerned with his prospect of going to college, and if I could have been that selfish, so would I have been. My cousins were the only ones to come by and spend some time with me. It was nice to have someone that you felt loved you enough to take the time and show you that it's ok. One of my cousins loved my cooking, so I cooked us some beef bbq ribs and macaroni and cheese. After I put D down after his feeding, we went outside, lit up, and mellowed out. Once we ate everyone went to sleep until a knock like the police awakened us. It was ok, it was my counselor bringing me my work so that I didn't get behind in school. I started working on the packet but honestly, I had no more interest in graduating. As a result, I didn't complete my work and decided against going back to TAPPs, so my mom registered me back in regular high school. My home school was different from my previous high school, but because I knew no one, it was a clean slate.

On my first day, my mom accompanied, and we sat down with my counselor and had a real conversation. She looked at my transcripts and saw my potential, but she also understood that having a child at my age would not be easy. She reminded me that while I had a great support system in place, I had to be the one to show up for me. While she was praising this "support system," I hoped she was right. At the end of her telling me all this, she stated that if I needed anything, not to hesitate to come and see her. As a 16-year-old, although I heard what she said, I had given up on people being there for me. I was used to being let down or walked away from, but not without first allowing myself to trust that person.

In my mind, I was now a woman, but I had no more idea of what that meant than when I was told that's what I was the first time. I was a child pretending I was in control of what I was doing but had no idea. I was stealing my mom's cigarettes and money if she wouldn't give it to me and skip school to go to Daniel's house. I tried so hard to make sure he didn't forget about me that I forgot about me. How was this a way to act as a parent or an adult? Wait, what am I thinking...this was what women do, right? Almost every woman I knew was putting their kids aside to keep some man in their life who meant them no good, and right now, I was no different. My son was in daycare learning ABC's, and here I was attempting to earn a PhD in stupid. Deeply I wanted to do the right thing, but I also wanted to feel love however it came. When I did attend school, I was not present. My mindset had changed, and now I felt school was a distraction. I was able to make one friend, but because I was so stuck on myself, I cannot remember much about her. What I do remember she was a freshman, who didn't think twice about befriending me. She and I became good school friends, but I wasn't up for opening myself up for a real friendship. It was better if she only saw the good in me. If I was honest with her, she would be honest with me, and I didn't want that. Of course, I didn't attend school regularly, and when I did, I didn't complete the necessary assignments. Finally, one day, my chemistry teacher asked, "Why do you come? You've missed so many days you cannot catch up". Those words would stick with me because they tore me up inside. To have another person dismiss my presence, although honestly, I was the one who stopped giving myself a chance to be seen, was upsetting. Instead of me recognizing what I had done wrong, I reacted. That was my queue and subsequently my last day in high school. After seeing my continued absences, my counselor reached out and asked why I had not been to school. I told her what he said, and she was outraged. "Why didn't you come to me," she asked. I gave her the same dumb answer I gave a little over nine months ago when I made another childish decision, "I don't know". That was the last time I spoke with her.

Now that I was a dropout, I spent more time at Daniel's house. He still attended school, but he had a treacherous side hustle selling drugs. I would love to say this was to help take care of his son, but if I needed something it was like pulling teeth. However, he did by him a blue Cadillac Sedan DeVille even though he didn't have any license. To give me some allies, I befriended the women of the neighborhood. They too had children and silent baby daddies. While they constantly asked why I don't go home, they taught me how to survive. They heard the conversations being had about me, but they didn't understand what I was going home to. You see it's easy to be around people who didn't like you, but you had no ties to rather than being around your blood and feeling the same way.

Although they were single parents, they were always dressed nice. Some of them received government assistance but since I couldn't because I wasn't old enough, I started boosting. At first it was just some things for D since Daniel wasn't thinking about it. Later it was myself and eventually I got a few things for Daniel. Although I never went anywhere, it was nice to look cute since I felt like crap. I rationalized it by saying whatever I thought made the most sense, but it didn't. To add to my disgust, I used my baby's diaper bag to put the merchandise in. Not only that, but I was also taking D with me while I was stealing as a cover. In the beginning, the adrenaline was awesome and then it became just something to do. It took me almost going to jail for me to understand that this was not the life for me.

When I began Kisha took me to the mall since they were grabbing things as well. When I ran my mouth and went outside the normal crew, was when it went south. Mary was new to the neighborhood, and I befriended her because she wasn't in Daniel's house. Trusting anyone in that house was hard because I was like the black sheep. I cannot understand why, but it was very evident. Because of this, I confided in her and allowed her into my so-called enterprise. Not only did she not know what she was doing, but for some reason, she thought I should steal for her so she wouldn't get caught... um, no, ma'am. As soon as she tried to put her stuff in my bag, unauthorized, she was spotted. OMG! I could not go to jail, but it was not looking good. The sales associate called security, and they were on the way. In the heat of the moment, I couldn't remember anything important, like how to get out or who I was with. Fight or flight kicked in, and my only goal was to figure out how I was going to get out of the mall without going to jail. Finally, I remembered that we were up, so I looked for steps or an escalator without attracting too much attention to myself. As I spotted the escalator, I just kept praying that if God got me out of there, I wouldn't steal anything else. As we started going down, I looked up only to see the salesperson pointing us out to security. We went from riding to running down the escalator since our mentality was if we were not in the store, they cannot search us. I made it unscathed but scarred and vowed that was my last time.

After what happened, I knew it was time I got a job. I took the first thing I could find, which was fast food. I wasn't making a lot of money, but it gave me a sense of maturity and independence. Sometimes, Daniel's mom would pick me up and drop me off, so I made sure I gave her something for that and living there on payday. Sometimes, it left me with just enough to buy pampers for D, but I was ok with that. Not long after, Keisha helped me get a job where she worked at Dress Barn, but the money was no better. They weren't busy, so I wasn't getting any hours. Finally, I secured a full-time position at Burlington Coat Factory at the same mall. While working was good, because I was no longer a full-time student, I lost the government subsidy keeping my son in daycare. This meant that I would have to find someone to take care of him while I was at work and Daniel was at school.

Unfortunately, D had a great sense of character and screamed as if someone were attacking him the moment, I stepped out the door. He was not discriminatory either because he would do this with Daniel, too. Although this broke my heart, it was the drawback of the life

I had created. What surprised me was the day Daniel had to ask his younger brother and sister to watch D while he went to take his exams. I cannot say what happened as the story changes depending on the person, but long story short, I received a frantic phone call that D wasn't breathing. I was livid and scared. There was no way for me to get there as quickly as I wanted, but I called a cab to get there as soon as possible. What had I done so wrong that something this dramatic happened to my child? I had to blame myself because my child was too innocent to have done anything that warranted this result. Now, I was upset with all parties involved and equally disgusted that Daniel allowed himself to be talked down from severely injuring the one who was being blamed for attempting to take my child's life. His sister had stated that his younger brother was alone with D when this happened. Had she not arrived and resuscitated my son by any means necessary, I would have been in jail. I truly believe that.

About a month later, Daniel dropped out of school. A few people were appalled because it was the end of the school year and closer to Daniel being a high school graduate. I'm sure it was all blamed on me, but truth be told, it was his negligence for school and his appreciation for the wrong life causing this issue. He had changed so much in the last six months that I wasn't sure we would last. His fascination for being the dope boy was showing. Now that he had so much extra time on his hands, the real holes started to show. Before I left West Meck, Daniel met and befriended Jim. He and I went to middle school ran track together. Unfortunately, I didn't know much about him but right off the bat he rubbed Kenya the wrong way. She overheard him speaking ill about me and that was it. Before Daniel dropped out, he started coming around and was now dating Megan. While I warned her that she was too good for him, just like me she heeded my advice.

Before his car broke down, Daniel dropped me off at work and supposedly kept D, although I doubt that seriously. He told me he would let D cry until he fell asleep, and after all the crying, D slept until it was time for me to get off. Part of this was probably because he was seeing some chic named Ke-Ke. He'd met her at school, and because she came after I left, I knew nothing about who she was. She must've been someone special because she would become a longtime pain in my derriere.

He always tried to hide things from me but was not good at it, so when I came across her number I didn't hesitate to call. I don't know what he told her, but she told me something that caused me to load some vengeance upon her. "You have a cute baby, "she said "What?!!" I replied. "This bitch has seen my baby?" I asked as he entered the room. Somehow, the two of them thought this was funny. He claimed she was lying. But she wasn't. He had a picture of D in his wallet, and she saw it. It didn't matter. This meant war in my eyes. I no longer wanted to fight her because of him but because she thought disrespecting me was cute. If he wanted to play games, then let's play. Just to be vindictive, I decided to visit my friend from the old neighborhood. I hadn't spoken to him since before I delivered the baby and against my better judgement I needed to get back at Daniel for Ke-Ke. D was at my mom's, and Daniel was nowhere to be found.

I made the mistake of taking Kisha. We found out that we were distant cousins, so I figured she had some loyalty. Little did I know, she was more focused on being a part of the inner circle and was only using me as a means to an end. We were forced to walk because her boyfriend and Daniel had her car. I didn't mind walking as it gave me time to think. Although we talked along the way, I appreciated the moments of silence that allowed me to process the relationships I had at Daniel's house. I felt like a fish out of water in that home, and honestly, it should've been my reason to go home. When we got to his house, I hugged him and introduced him to her. We had a short conversation before I decided I was ready to go. I went to prove that I could have someone else if I wanted. The issue was I was afraid that if I left, he would do much less to help me take care of D, and I would be alone.

On the way back, she thought telling me how much better he was for me than Daniel was amusing. It was gaslighting at its finest, so I brushed it off as innocent girl talk. My intuition told me she was a traitor before we left, so I wasn't hearing her. When we returned, I stayed outside for a minute while she went inside the house. Low and behold, she went to tell his sisters everything about our trip. I was unaware of what happened until Daniel came back. They quickly took him aside and spilled what they thought was tea. It wasn't long before he was yelling at me as I sat there speechless. Although I was afraid of what was going to happen, I did my best to defend that nothing happened. He demanded that I take him over there, but I wouldn't. What I didn't count on was Kisha's loyalty to them and she would.

He demanded I get in the car. I was so mad I thought, who does something like this? It was conclusive that I was on an island alone in my life. There was no one looking out for me; they were just people looking to take away my happiness. This guy was a friend to me. Someone neutral from the bullshit I had to deal with, and now that was about to be taken away. This clown was able to screw anything that moved, and no one said a word. I understood that if I wanted to befriend him, I should've gone home, but if he wanted to cheat, he should've broken up with me. When we pulled up, I was too ashamed to get out. This was a man, and it was childish to come to his home with mess. He came outside, confused about what was going on. As I stood beside the car with the look of fear on my face, I could tell he felt sympathy towards what I was going through. He tried convincing Daniel nothing was going on, but as Daniel stared into my soul, I could tell he didn't believe him.

"Get your ass in the car" he said once he didn't get the response he wanted. As soon as we turned the corner, smack! He slapped my face so hard I heard ringing in my ears. "Stop the car", he told her "No," I rebuttled, but she wanted to see me get my ass whooped so she did exactly what he told her to do. He came around to my side as I was hollering, "Why did you stop?" and she continued to look stupid.

He opened the door and started hitting me again before his brother warned him that people could see and would call the police. He got back in the car, but the arguing continued as I cried the entire time. Once we arrived back at the house, I jumped out of the car and ran into the house with him running behind me to continue putting his hands on me. As I sat in the room crying, I had so many emotions running through me that the tears were full of betrayal, hurt, anger, and embarrassment, just to name a few. I knew then I could trust only myself. Truthfully, I should never have expected her to keep my secret; that was my fault. She was trying to get into the family and would do whatever, but I was not. After that, I mostly stayed in the house out of embarrassment because I knew I could trust no one. I should've gone home.

By June 1998, I was immune to my life. Whatever I felt about it I pushed down so far even I didn't recognize who I had become. Not only was my love life a mess, but I'd lost my job. Unknowingly Sharon was out stealing, and I noticed her on my way to lunch. After our small talk I left as my mom had stopped by to take me to lunch. When I returned, they were hauling her off to jail and fired me for knowing her claiming I helped. If I had helped her, she wouldn't have gotten caught, but I took my loss and left. It was fine because it allowed me to spend more time with D.

Daniel's life had taken a turn, and his drug dealing became reckless. So, on that hot day in June when I heard that he had been arrested, I was not surprised. I was in the house taking D a bath when they yelled what was happening. He was being chased by the police for riding in a "stolen vehicle". Honestly it wasn't stolen but someone who was done smoking crack and now wanted their car. Had I been thinking, I should've gotten on the bus and let him figure it out, but instead, I went to see what happened. I left D at home while I went to stand by my man like any other oblivious girl would do. His sister was already there, and I joined in on cussing and showing out when the police arrested us both for inciting a riot. His mom came to voice her opposition, and they kept the arrest going and collected her as well. As I sat in that car, I thought, what in the world made me think this was ok. What was I doing here instead of being home with my child? Would either one of them have come down if it were me? It didn't matter because now I was handcuffed and was on my way to jail. I hoped someone took care of D because I didn't make sure he was ok before I thoughtlessly went down there. They lied to us and said we were not going to jail and would be given a slap on the wrist. They put me, his mom, and sister back in the police car and drove us back to the neighborhood, but only let out his sister. I was booked but allowed to sign myself out by the magistrate. I left happy yet sad because I knew Daniel was not getting out with me.

When we got back to the neighborhood, the first person I needed to see was D. After I hugged my son and got him ready for bed, I went out on the porch to recollect what just happened. As I sat there smoking my Newport, I wondered why it tasted funny. Immediately, I gave it away because it was making me sick to the stomach. A few days later, I found out I was pregnant again. What?! I only meant to get pregnant once, not twice, but it was too late. How was I going to explain this to Daniel? Better yet, my mom? Whatever I needed to do, I had to get him out. I tried selling weed, but I was no good at it. I probably made my money plus a few dollars, but it was nowhere near what I needed to get him out. I wanted to work but had no one to care for D. This was a complete mess. His parents contemplated getting him out until the police raided the home, and they were taken to jail. The police had no case, but that didn't stop them from coming in, guns drawn, telling us to get down, and tearing up the place. I was upstairs, and I had just finished taking D a bath when I heard, "get down, get down". I turned around, and there were two men with big guns pointed in my face. They told me to get down on the floor, but D was screaming his head off. They couldn't care less and just kept saying get down before they shoot. I complied and was placed in handcuffs yet again, but this time in front of my child. After they checked the room, they allowed me to get him so he would stop crying. This was not a life I was accustomed to and definitely not one I needed to raise a child around. His parents probably felt the same way as they were working parents, and what was going on was nothing they had shown their kids.

Now that Daniel was in jail, I figured I should try to graduate. Since this was the only place I could talk to Daniel, I chose to stay here. My mom didn't like D being here, so it wasn't hard for me to convince her to keep him. The only obligation was I had to make sure I came to get him on the weekends. This time I needed to get it right. Here I was 17 on baby number two and there was nothing I could offer either of them. In the beginning, I did well and was sure I could finish. It wasn't long before I was missing days and once he was released, quit again. This was my secret until my mom dropped off D and Daniel's dad told her both that I had quit and pregnant again. I was so confused as to why he did that. At the time, I thought he just wanted me to go home, but now I think that, as a father, he saw that this was not who I was and that I needed to go home. Immediately she demanded I come home and get my baby, and I couldn't blame her. A month after he got out, his parents said they were moving, and no one was going except his sisters. It took some doing, but my mom said that Daniel could come live with us. He didn't want to and was still dope dealing, so he stayed in the Bahamas until the last possible moment. I wish I had let him stay and moved on. He was supposed to be the safe person for me which made him the worst person at times. Again, I say, when you know someone hates you it doesn't matter but when the ones who say they love you don't, it hurts.

Reality Check

Getting Daniel to finally come to my mom's was probably my greatest task. I often wondered if he blamed me for not being able to go with his mom. Years later, I debunked that theory when I learned that Daniel does what Daniel wants to do. His dad realized that as well which backed his decision. Once he arrived, you could cut the tension in the house with a knife. It was obvious that Daniel and my mom did not like one another. Somehow, they were both upset for how I was being treated yet were to blame for it. I thought they were both fighting for control because if one didn't want me to put up with their bs, it was the other one. Later I found out that it was partly the secrets the two of them knew about one another that kept them at odds. The thought that either one of them wanted me to choose them was almost comical. My hope was he would take this time to spend with D, but I don't think he knew how. I felt his aggression towards me was keeping him from addressing his responsibility. On top of that, I found out that not only was my mom charging us to stay, which was understandable, but she woke him up and demanded free drugs too. I can imagine how this would make a person frustrated.

Finally, Daniel secured a job through a temp agency at Eckerd's Warehouse. Although I was happy for him, it wouldn't be long before he was back to his shenanigans. He hardly came home after work since his mom got off around the same time. She would pick him up to go to their house. For whatever reason, I couldn't understand why I didn't see this as a good thing. This meant less of a silent hostile environment and more time for me to figure out life. It wasn't long before he convinced his mom and dad to let him come home. Because he worked up the street from the house, sometimes he'd stop by while he waited for his mom to pick him up. Occasionally, he would allow D and me to join him, but I never felt welcome. While this should have stopped me from going, it didn't. This happens when you invest your life in someone before you understand what it is like to live. Their pure existence drives you; without it, you don't feel whole. By this time everyone had their mates here yet somehow, I felt like I was being singled out. Their father tried to help me understand their allegiance to their own. He too became enraged with what was happening but would just leave. At the time I took what he said with a grain of salt because there were times he was included.

This baby was taking its sweet time to make an entrance. We were already two weeks past the due date with no baby. Although I experienced Braxton hicks, the doctors refused to keep and induce me. Every time I went to the ER and was sent home it infuriated him as if I had control of what was happening. As a result, when the real-time came, I was met with a hard "NO" when I asked if he was going to the hospital with me. Therefore, I sat there in pain while he continued getting ready for work. Inside, I was boiling like a pot of grits, but waited patiently to ask his mom. I wiped the tears from my eyes as I sat in the back of his mom's Escort GT, clinching my leg as the labor pains continued to grow in intensity. While he took D in the house, I leaned over and asked his mom to drop me off at the hospital. Since she was a mom, my hope was she felt my urgency but replied that she had to get ready for work first. Consequently, it didn't matter because once my mom saw how much pain I was in, she called 911, and we went by ambulance. Since this was the real deal, I called him to join us. His response revealed no sense of urgency but thankfully a coworker overheard and brought him during lunch. Finally, he arrived just a few short hours before we welcomed our second son, Davion. While trying to bask in the joy of childbirth, I went unconscious. All I could hear was the doctors putting everyone out of the room and calling my name, trying to keep me conscious as they tried to save my life. You would've thought that would have awakened the people around me but nah. I woke up in my recovery room, and everyone was gone. They brought Davion down to see me, and he was the light I had never known I needed. Daniel and I had already chosen his name, but when it was time to solidify that name with our signatures, he never showed up. I was unaware of what was going on and why he was acting so distant. Unfortunately, it didn't end with him.

Being that my mom didn't have a car, I was tasked with asking Daniel's mom to pick me up from the hospital. While Daniel was not there to see us home, he was thoughtful to brace us with his presence after work and stay the night. While I was happy about the help, I was curious to find out why he was going out of his way to give us his butt to kiss. Against my better judgement, I reduced my healing time and returned to the lion's den. Although I could smell the deceit as soon as I got out of the car, I told myself I was overthinking. Instead, I said that if I got a job, it would help the way they saw me. Davion was barely six weeks before I was looking for employment.

Megan and Kisha got me an interview at Burger King, where they worked. To help you understand the level of jealousy I dealt with from all those close to me would take the rest of my life because it never stopped. Although we were all working for the EXACT same place that wouldn't buy us anything worth speaking of, Kisha didn't want me to ride with them because I made $6.50 whereas they made $6.25. Not only that, but I had to beg my mom to watch the children. I was hopeful she would be pleased with me for trying to do for my children, but that was not conveyed. Kisha and Megan were always late because Kisha was always doing unnecessary begging with Daniel's brother, so I caught the bus and rode back with them. It was challenging sitting in the back seat, trying to act as if I didn't hear Kisha mumbling. She was so fixated on me that there was no reason to say anything as long as that mumbling stayed a mumble. It was hard enough for her that she could never be me, no matter how hard she tried. A few days later, Megan convinced Kisha that I should ride with them to work, and while I appreciated her for getting me a ride, it was unwarranted. That same day Kisha was fired, and she was not happy. Her attitude was always unnecessary, and they had about enough of it. While she continued to take us to work in a dangerous hurry, I focused on the conversation I had with the manager. He spoke to me about a leadership role for which I was all too thankful. Eager to get home and tell my mom, she stopped me and told me she had a job that starts Monday so she could no longer babysit.

What! I had no idea that she was looking let alone deciding to start asap. My children were definitely not her responsibility but some kind of notice would've helped. There was no reason to argue because her mind was made up. As I sat on the couch as she continued drinking and rationalizing her decision I wondered when my time was coming. While I was pregnant, I reconnected with my dad who was getting out soon. Maybe he and I could get a place, but I knew that was a long shot. So, it was back to playing a stay-at-home single mom because Daniel was useless. As usual, I waited until he got off and went to feel like an outcast at his mom's. Usually, I sat in the kitchen with his mom, learning what it meant to be a woman and a wife while they watched 106 & Park and played the PlayStation. Sometimes I joined in but kept my distance. Out of all his foolery, Daniel had the audacity to be jealous, so I was careful. He allowed me to braid Jacob, his brother, and Jim's hair until Jim decided he wanted to cause problems. While I braided Jacob's hair he blurted out "dang Brandy we were cool when Daniel was locked up, now you have changed". This couldn't be further from the truth but no one in this group wanted truth because secretly no one liked me. There was nothing that changed in our dynamic other than my jealous, abusive, baby daddy was home, and I knew better. I couldn't understand how and why my name was brought up in almost everything. I had so much power just by walking into a room with them, but on the inside, I was broken into 1000 pieces.

Of course, those words encouraged Daniel to look at me sideways. Anytime I went back, I stayed in the kitchen with his mom until I left. While Jim was pointing the finger at me, he was up to some behavior that didn't sit well with the family. Word had gotten back to their family that he was abusing Megan. My heart went out to her because I understood what she was going through, but Daniel decided he wasn't going to allow this happen. She was still spending time with him oblivious that her secret was out in the open. When they pulled up, Daniel went out the door and slapped the taste out of his mouth. Now, for me, this was a joke for two reasons. One, Daniel was doing the same thing to me, and no one batted an eye as if I deserved it, and two, he didn't think about what if my family knew he was hitting me. Honestly when he slapped him, he slapped me too. What he didn't plan for was Megan to defend him and tell him to leave. This was astonishing to watch. When they arrived at their destination, Megan called back unappreciative of what just happened. Instead of Jim keeping his mouth shut, he didn't, and so against better judgment, Daniel and his brother went to where he was to finish the score. Apparently, he too had called some people which concluded that this wouldn't end well. Daniel's mom and I went behind them to hopefully keep things from escalating. There was a bunch of back and forth before his mom became fearful for her son and felt like she needed to insert herself. Now let's be clear, I had nothing to do with the fight, nor was I saying anything while everything went down. So, when I was brought to center stage, I couldn't understand the motive. "You need to be worried about why Brandy is sleeping with my son," his mom belted out. Everyone stopped at that moment and turned around to look at me. WHAT IN THE WORLD!! I was so stunned that I couldn't say a word. I stood there with my mouth wide open, and all I could do was shake my head no. Apparently, this was the second time I was accused of this action. The first would be while Daniel was in jail. I was home from school one day, and Jim was there. I can't remember why, but he chased me outside. Word got back, and I was now accused of sleeping with him. Next, the guy's mom accused me because later I found out he was with a Brandy just not me. Incidentally a conspiracy was born and now there was doubt that Davion was Daniels. Now things were making sense as to why Davion wasn't embraced like D. Now the side eyes and whispering made sense to me; they all believed I had done so, but no one had the guts to say anything.

After what happened, I tried to convince Daniel that nothing happened. While I was outcasted, Jim was embraced and never questioned if this ever occurred. He and Daniel carried on never truly skipping a beat. How unbelievably stupid I felt everyone was who believed he deserved to be forgiven. Unfortunately, this is how it's usually done when a woman is accused of doing something, and NO ONE takes time to believe the man lied. So, instead of my man standing up for me and defending my honor, what does he do? He fell in line with the rest of the cackling hens and played judge, jury, and executioner to my character. After this event, Daniel became even more callous than usual. He was waiting for the right opportunity to unleash the anger and embarrassment from the lies. After one of many arguments about this, he slapped me, and I took my kids and decided to walk home in the dark. This was dangerous, but I would have been even more in danger if I had stayed. He followed me arguing and hitting me as if my goal was to fight instead of de-escalating the situation. Unfortunately, he had been drinking so he was ready for this and made sure I couldn't fight back. As I held Davion in my arms and D by the hand in silence so as not to agitate the situation further, he slapped me with everything he had. The more I tried to leave, the more he hit me. He knew I was defenseless because I had the children, but that didn't stop him. He wanted me to fight him to give him a reason to hit me harder, but I just wanted to get my kids safely home. Just then, he took them both from me. They were crying, I was crying, and this evil person couldn't care less. At first, I tried to grab them but when he drew back to hit me again, I withdrew. I let him walk away with them to keep them safe from any more drama. As I walked the five miles home, my vision was impaired due to the strikes from him and the tears from me. Quietly I entered the house so that no one saw my face. If it looked half as bad as I felt on the inside, I was right to spare myself the extra judgement.

Waking up the next day wasn't easy but necessary. While I was beaten and bruised, I wanted my kids away from this person. This was the perfect opportunity to say I'm done yet I wasn't ready to make that decision. Was this who I was going to be? A woman who stayed even when she was being hurt in every way possible. Although the answer to that question now is hell no, the light inside me was barely shining at that time so this was who I became. My mom was upset when she saw my face, but it was too late to knock some sense into me. Now my answer to anything he did was, "but I know he love me". He had me wrapped around his finger because I was afraid to stand up and believe in me. Here, I thought he was my savior but found out I would have to save myself. Before I left to get the boys, I called to try and ease the tension. There was no hope. I was bitch this and bitch that which is the go-to name for every abuser to beat you emotionally, and it was working. Even though I was fearful, I was going to get my children. A family friend had stopped by and was eager to help by taking me to get them. Instead of someone saying something, everyone stood by and spectated as we argued about getting my children. I hope I never become the type of woman who sits back and watches a man treat another woman that way. My mom tried to help but eventually I told her to let me handle it. She was only making a bad situation worse. Reluctantly, he told Davion to go, but not without saying, "he probably isn't mine anyway." How hurtful and in front of our kids. He held on to D and said he wasn't going anywhere. I cried, got in the car, and left to keep the peace. The fight in me was gone, and it was clear I had some work to do to regain what was in me. It didn't worry me that physically, I may not be able to beat him, but mentally and emotionally I had to regain. The next day, he called me to get D, which I figured he would because being a father full-time was something he couldn't manage.

After he was alone again, he decided to call and apologize. Of course, I was the reason it escalated as he needed someone to be the blame. After work, he stopped by pretending to play with the children, but I knew it was a ploy to get me. While I did conditionally take him back, I decided it was time I stay home. There was nothing for me being at Daniel's house; it was time I poured more into myself and my children. Recently I signed up for the work first program which gave me $272/month, but I had to work a certain number of hours. My mom told me about a position at a sandwich shop near where she worked. The position wasn't fulltime, but through the program I could get the check and automatically receive ChildCare Resources. This was great because I could put the boys back in daycare. Although I only worked a few hours, I made the best of it as it gave me a sense of pride. Anytime I needed anything, the owner was willing to help, and I was appreciative. Daniel's mom had signed for him a car, so he took me to get the boys from daycare when he got off. We finally formed a well-oiled machine that was helpful to both of us. Whatever he gave, I was taking if it meant getting the boys what they needed. This job was only $175/week, so I wasn't getting rich, but it was preparing me for better.

We were happily coexisting, but this came with consequences. After I got my license, Daniel started allowing me to drive and I would pick him up. It was a warehouse, so they all got off at the same time. Slowly I started seeing girls talking and giggling with one mean mugging me, but I overlooked it. I thought it was them considering me lucky and I was but not because of him. As it became more frequent my gut knew there was something going on, but I couldn't prove it. Before I wouldn't have reacted, but I was over that. If he wanted to go that was up to him. What they failed to realize, even though I constantly told them, you can have him, I'm not holding him, but he won't leave.

Unfortunately, he told them that he was leaving me, so when I received a phone call at work, it was not surprising. "Hi, my name is Tasha, and I'm sleeping with your man," she said. What in the world was this now? The disrespect was now on another level. "How do you know me?" I asked. "I got your number from his phone," she said. "I would see you when you came to pick him up," she bolstered. Oh wow! I thought. This was nauseating to me. I remember getting mean-mugged by some chic as I picked him up. I didn't pay any mind to it because I had no reason. I was naïve in thinking nothing of it because why would this girl take the time to mean mug me and didn't know me? That night, I received another daunting phone call. It was her. "Hello," I answered "It's her" the person said, and they hung up. Hmmm, I thought. I tried to *69, a way to call people back, but she blocked her number before she called, so it wouldn't work. The bad thing about drama is that it doesn't stop until it has drained the life out of you. That's why I knew it was her when the phone rang again before I answered. "Hello," I answered, aggravated. "He's here", she said, "say something. Tell her you're here," she told whoever was there. The person didn't say anything, but I knew exactly who she was referring to. Immediately, I hung up and called Daniel.

This phone call resulted in the worst cat-and-mouse game I have ever played. It was worse than when Brandy was at his house. By now, I had slept beside this man for years, and I knew his moves better than anyone, but still, his family attempted to play me like a fool. First, he was gone to the store. Then he was sleeping, then they stopped answering the phone altogether. So, what did I do? I caught a cab to see this shamble of lies for myself. When I arrived, there was no Daniel, and I received another lie. He just left. I was aggravated, so I went home. As soon as I got home, he called and played as if he knew nothing. The next day, I went to work and received yet another phone call. "Hello" I answered, "Hey, it's Tasha. Your boyfriend took my stuff," she said. "Wait, wait, wait. You sleep with my boyfriend, call me to boast about it, try to get him caught, it backfires, and now you call me because he took something from you". "I'm sorry for what has happened to you, but don't call my phone about this. I must get back to work, and I don't have anything to do with you and him," I replied and hung up. She called back, and I hung up. After she called the last time, she ended by telling me she thought I should know, which was a lie because if so, why wait until you are upset to tell me? I picked him up almost daily, so she had plenty of time to say something instead of mean-mugging me. Just then, I remembered who she was because she was always rolling her eyes, and when I asked him why, he proclaimed he didn't know. "Well, look, I must get back to work, and I have nothing to do with what y'all are going through. Don't call me anymore, and good luck", I said as I ended the phone call.

Recently someone asked me, "How was he allowed to do this to you? You don't take this kind of behavior". I answered them by saying, "Before and after him, you are exactly right, but somehow; he had put a fear in me I could not overcome. This allowed me to be so quick to take him back knowing his apologies were empty." I know this because it was only a matter of time before I was faced with the next girl claiming he wanted her. I cannot say I was a saint, but I didn't deserve this. I hoped he stayed with one of them, but he always returned because I allowed him to. To quote the movie "What's Love Got To Do With It", I knew what it felt like to have your family walk out on you, and I just couldn't walk out.

{ 8 }

Moving Day

Although I couldn't deduce what this woman's motive was for calling me, I wasn't going to let this get me fired. My boss, Sara, was a small, framed woman from Vietnam who smoked Capri cigarettes. Although she was soft, her words were filled with a heaviness that let you know she meant business. Therefore, I had to find a way to keep my drama at a minimum while I worked. During our downtime, we discussed life and mine, and she vowed to help me in any way she could. She already helped me tell Childcare Resources that I worked 30 hours so I could get them into daycare. This made my life a lot easier as I could go to work and not worry who would take care of my children that day. As I settled into my position, my cousin Sharon approached me about a job. My boss wasn't looking for anyone, but she hired her because I had asked her to. This was the same cousin that had cost me my job a few years earlier. In my mind, I questioned why I was helping someone who had cost me my job before. For some, they would've said "heck no" but I had forgiven her and wanted to help. Not only did I get her the job, but I also cut my days so that it would be financially viable for my boss. But in the true fashion of anyone given something they didn't earn; she took it for granted. My boss was complaining about her coming in and talking on the phone excessively, and just like that, she was fired. While I was sorry to see anyone lose their job, I was happy to have my hours back. Unfortunately, my hours would stay the same as business was not as affluent as it once was. I had only been here a few months, but Sarah was right when she stated it was time, I found something that could provide me with more money. Since I was notified that I wouldn't have a job soon, I began looking for a new position. Luckily, I found a job at Carolinas Medical Center in the cafeteria as a cashier. I was 18 years old by this time and decided I also needed my own place, for which Sarah provided me with payroll information.

Finally, my life was moving in a positive direction. We had our own place, and although it was on the street next to his parents' place, I could not care less. It was a peace of mind being able to come home, and there was no one drinking and cussing excessively or looking at me in disgust. Daniel's mom was kind enough to cosign our new furniture from Kimbrell's Furniture. I wanted to furnish the entire house, but Daniel was not helping me with the payments. Instead, he convinced me that the boys could sleep on the mattress pads we slept on while at his mom's. Reluctantly, I agreed since I had no other options. His mom had already made it clear that this was her credit, so she wanted to make sure I could pay for what I was getting. As long as my children had a home, I was content. I promised myself that as soon as I paid off this debt, I would get them the bed they deserved.

Everyone was at our house on move-in day, mostly spectators. You can always tell who your fake supporters are when you get something new. They say they're happy for you just before they say what they would've done differently. I know because I have been one. When I saw the smiles on my children's faces, I let the haters hate and continued enjoying my new independence. Daniel was a felon, so everything was in my name, and I was ok with that. If anything happened and he left, I was able to take care of my place on my own. At least, that's what I was telling myself. In the meantime, I felt like I was taking back my life. When I walked through that threshold I vowed never to go home or anyone else's home again. Though I was ecstatic about having my own place, I would miss trying to have a place at home with my mom. Whatever was keeping us from having the mother-daughter relationship while I was home was now going to be challenged with me living in my own place. Camila was sad to see us go because she had developed a close relationship with D and Davion. As we drove away, I hoped that my mom would reflect on her life and see this as a plea for her to get herself together. I also questioned if the person I was walking away with had my best interest at heart. I would have much rather stayed home if finally, I could feel the love my mom used to have for me.

My dad was released and made seeing us his first stop. He decided he didn't want to stay but instead move back to Winston-Salem. Since my mom was having a hard time with Camila, she convinced my dad that he should take her with him. Honestly, we both needed to go but I already had my place. Funny how life works because within a month my dad relapsed, replaced in custody with another charge in Charlotte, Camila was in a bad accident, and we found out she was expecting a child. Of course, I interrogated my mom about what was she going to do who responded very differently. There was no talk of "abortion", but she had to support her. Although I was flabbergasted this wasn't about me and truth be told I made my decision. After my sister healed from her wounds, my mom sent her to a place for pregnant teens, Florence Crittenton. I don't know if she was embarrassed that both her daughters were teenage moms. Camila was only able to come home on the weekends, so sometimes I picked her up so we could spend time together. While I was angry at her, I realized some of my actions caused her reactions, so I shared some of the blame. Because she looked up to me, I should have been a better example, but I didn't know how.

Working the second shift at the hospital became an issue. I dropped Daniel off in the morning so I could take the boys to daycare. Before work, I had to drop the car back off so he could pick up the boys, and I caught the bus to work. When I got off at 11, Daniel picked me up and it messed with the boy's sleep schedule. After two weeks, I requested to go to third shift. This was the first time I'd worked third shift, and if I have it my way, my last. During the week, I drove, but when it got to the weekend, Daniel wanted the opportunity to run the streets. Mostly, he left the boys at his mom's when he went out, which I was never a fan of. For whatever reason, I never felt like they were cared for the way I wanted them to be. That's not to say they were mistreated, but my trust was gone. Quickly I became friends with my manager, April. April was a stocky, brown-skinned woman who stood 5'0. Though she was no-nonsense, she was compassionate at the same time. Everyone respected her whether they liked her or not. She taught me a lot about more than just being a cashier, and it bloomed into a friendship. So much so that she hired Megan, at my asking. It was convenient she worked there whenever Daniel neglected to take or pick me up.

Slowly our house turned into the house I was running away from. Now we were drinking until we were drunk, or Daniel went to the club. He'd made it clear that I wasn't allowed to go out, so I went to sleep. He also attempted to alienate me from my family because he was fearful, they would introduce me to someone. IF ONLY! His brother and childhood friends would fill up the house on Friday and Saturday nights. Sometimes Kisha and Megan came down, but usually I was the only woman there. None of the men brought their women, who were probably experiencing my same afflictions. There was always a scowl on my face as I just wanted one weekend to relax and be some sort of family. Watch a movie or, better yet, go to the movies or go out on a date. When we did, we were almost always accompanied by another couple. I found out that this was so Daniel could lie that he was not with me if he was seen by some girl he was messing with. This came from inside his camp, who loved having pillow talk with his girlfriend. I learned to be ok with the partying as I enjoyed drinking myself if it didn't lead into a fight. Fearfully I made plans to hang with April since he made it clear this was my life. My hope was he saw how innocent it could be and be ok with it, but it was a longshot.

In The Damn Way

April asked me if I wanted to go to the movies and out to eat. I didn't have ANY girlfriends, so this was something new for me. Emily and I lost touch after the move, so I were alone unless I was with his family. She volunteered to pick me up because I knew Daniel would not let me drive. It was a Saturday afternoon, so I was eager to get out. As I got dressed, slowly his mood changed, and I became anxious. Because we were going in broad daylight, I was hopeful this wouldn't heighten. When April walked in, I could tell she felt the vibe by the look in her eyes. I decided to have a cocktail before she arrived, and I offered her one. My hope was to calm down, but it was unsuccessful. We sat down, as Daniel was back and forth, mumbling as if he was convincing himself to go nuclear. Just then, that mumble changed to a conversation filled with derogatory words and threats. At first, they were just at me, but as soon as April came to my defense, he started in on her. She was not the one and stood to her defense, ready for what-ever Daniel thought he was going to do. What he didn't know is that she had a pistol and was not afraid to use it. After a few minutes, she said enough was enough and that she was leaving. Just as I apologized for what was happening, he dashed his entire drink on me that soaked my hair and clothes before saying, "You ain't going no f**king where". Fearful that he would use that gun I knew he had, I sat there in em-barrassment. As a result, that was the last time I had any friend girl over or made plans to hang out.

As I look back, I sometimes try to understand what about me drove this man to such lengths. Not only that, but how these individuals, mostly men, groom women to stay long after the abuse begins. Honestly, I feel that generationally, we have been conditioned to beat or be beaten, abuse or be abused and stay. Over time, I learned to be okay with not having any friends. Besides, my mom moved a couple of streets over, so sometimes, my sister would stop by. She had given birth to my nephew but was not ready to be a parent. Instantly my mom became his caretaker while Camila continued having fun. Strangely when Camila stopped by, I wasn't always happy to see her. To my face, I felt like she was an ally, but deep down, I felt like she would turn on me for Daniel. Oddly he and her had a better relationship that felt weird. Although this is something I have never said until now, I was always jealous of how she could get what she wanted from him. She was only around 14 at the time and was asking for a ride and money to go skating, and he was always willing to give her what she asked for. This was poison pulsing through my veins because of everything I had gone through with this man. He told me it was because of me that he did for her, but I never could understand that. Often, I was happy to see my family, even if they did want something. Family was the only kryptonite that kept him calm, at least until they left. Sometimes, I tried to keep them around longer because I could tell if things were going to go left once, they were gone. Because we shared the bills I had to be just as graceful when his family came around. It was not as easy for me because not all his family had good intentions. So, when his cousin begins coming around, my spidey senses went off continuously.

We had been together four years, and this was the first time I'd met any cousins from his father side of the family. Although I heard about them, I wanted to believe they weren't as bad. Anyway, my family had a dark side so how different could this be. Little did I know he and Daniel's evilness was cut from the same cloth. This became evident when he sat there while Daniel put his hands on me, laughing. This time, I called my mom, and while they were disrespectfully cussing while I was on the phone, she told me she was coming to get me. Because I knew how that would end, I told her I was walking, and she could meet me. She and my aunt met me at the store. Although I could smell what they had been doing, I did my best to put that behind me. Immediately, she called 911, and while this was common on Beatties Ford Rd., I was embarrassed that it was me they were coming for. The police took pictures and asked if I wanted to press charges. My aunt and mom were quick to holler "Yep," and they were right to do so. Slowly, I agreed in hopes of finally getting him to stop. The police immediately left to arrest him for domestic abuse. This was the first time I had heard this term. Until that night, I considered our confrontations a fight, but we weren't the ones with the beef. He was.

My feelings about him getting arrested were 50/50. It was too late to change my mind because now they had evidence. My fear was this was going to start another fight. They returned empty-handed, as Daniel hid in the woods, as his cousin politely lied for him. There's nothing worse than someone who's already a loose cannon with an enabler. The police recommended that I go to my mom's house for the night, but I knew Daniel would be leaving soon, as it was time for the club. Slowly, I walked home and hid until he left. As I walked through the door, I remembered the day I said yes to this place. It had so much life and potential, but that feeling had slowly been erased. All I could see were the arguments, drinking, fighting, and makeup sex that felt like the only thing holding us together. There was no love in here other than the love I mustered to give to my children. That night, I slept loosely on the couch just in case he came home ready for round two. When he arrived, he was too inebriated to fuss and proceeded to go to bed into the bedroom. Time passed, and, on a technicality, he was finally arrested and charged with domestic abuse.

By this time, we had made up, and things were going "good". So, when he was arrested for the other charge, I did my best to get the bond money together, only to find out he was on a mandatory 72-hour hold. This is where a classic case of "victimizing the victim" came into play. No one wanted to find out why he hit me. It was more how could I allow this to happen to their brother and son. TF!! How was this my fault? The crazy part is he was doing the same thing when he called. The sane part of me was saying leave him in there and let them figure it out since they are blaming you. Unfortunately, Monday came, and I was right there when it was time for him to get out. There was no use as he was still upset about me pressing charges to begin with. Confused as to how he had become the victim, I played along. Because of his demeanor, I figured the way to make this go away is if I didn't go to court. It didn't matter because I was summoned and had no choice. The day of court, he was intimidating me to drop everything so his charges would be dismissed. What about me? He had abused me, broken my trust, and caused me fear, but because of those things I was also willing to do what he said. I felt weak that even in court, with the judge and police on my side, he was able to put the fear of God in me. My lawyer asked what happened, and I told the truth. She said they could get him anger management, which was good. Tactfully, his lawyer told him there would be jail time, and he was upset AGAIN.

We were both being represented by women, yet the woman representing him felt the need to allow my abuser to victimize me yet again. Although I began by telling the truth, it was time to lie as I had no choice if I wanted peace. So, I got up on the stand and LIED. I altered the story and made me the aggressor and him the victim. My lawyer and the judge were taken aback, and both lit into me. Single-handedly I took away my chances for this to stop and instead enabled him to continue abusing me. Because I lied, the judge sentenced me for "endangerment of children" since I was reluctant to end what was happening. Most people would have been devastated, but I was thankful, in the end, for my social worker. She got me much-needed house supplies and things for my children before she closed my case. I was sad to see her go because her presence allowed peace over our house. It was the only time when we were on our best behavior because we never knew when she would come. On her last day, she was able to have a conversation with Daniel and explained the importance of family. I hoped he heard her and would change. Truly, I was tired of arguing, fighting, and making up because he was caught up with some female or he didn't like something I said or did. Growing up, I saw enough dysfunctional relationships to know that I was ready to turn this page and do something different.

Now that we were cleared of the judicial system threatening to take the kids, it was business as usual. Our many altercations became a burden on my performance and attendance at work. Because of the many callouts for various reasons, I was at risk of losing my job. Some of those reasons involved him not wanting to take or pick me up from work. Since there was only one car, the final decision was usually his. Unfortunately, I wasn't making enough for a car payment, so I had to suck it up begrudgingly. By this time, we were coexisting, and I had taken the mattress off the bed and moved it into the living room. However, it wasn't long before we were in another altercation. It usually began with him drinking and reliving something that was previously handled. While I sat on the bed listening to him go on and on about nothing, I thought about the mound of clothes I was going to wash the next day. As my mind drifted, I was surprised when he approached me and started choking me. That was another thing that drove him mad, the fact that I ignored him. As he choked me, I tried to grab something to get him off me. Hopeful that there was something on this bed other than clothes. I had to act fast as I could feel myself slipping into unconsciousness. When I pulled my hand up with the object, I realized it was a knife. I thought I could kill him right now, and this would all be over with. The issue was I didn't want to kill him, but I wanted to hurt him, so I took the strength I had left and struck him. "Ahhhhhhhhh!" he screamed and let go. Dazed, I lifted my head, not knowing I was right below the top glass of the table and struck my eye. My adrenaline was pumping so hard because, for the first time he felt what it was like to have someone strike you. Not only that, but I also wanted to see what damage I had caused. Omg! There was blood gushing everywhere as I stabbed him in the thigh. Afraid of him hurting me worse now that I had finally hurt him, I tried to get the blood to stop. It wasn't working, so I had to get some first aid equipment. I asked him to drive his car, but his pride had been attacked, and he was not going to assist me, although he was the one who needed help. As I walked the street to the CVS, I smiled that ultimately, I had taken some stance at defending myself. I was doing what I had to do to keep my children from being taken, was what I told myself. The thought of going to jail was not an option, and I was certain he would send me there. When I returned,

I did my best to help, but he didn't want it. I had challenged his authority, and while he was upset, I was at peace.

When I woke up the next morning and took a hard look at myself in the mirror, I noticed something was off. The striking from the table had produced a black eye. "Oh crap," I thought. How was I going to go to work like this? My job was already hanging in the balance, and I knew I could potentially lose my job if I missed tonight. "Forget it," I said to myself. There was no way I was going to let anyone else know what I was dealing with at home. It was embarrassing enough to go through this, but to have people I don't know staring at me, I couldn't have that. I learned from the last time that putting raw steak on my eye would help. Unfortunately, that didn't work instantly as I had anticipated. So, I called the manager on duty to say I wouldn't be there that night. Once I knew April was at work, I called to tell her what happened. "Wow", she said, "why didn't you call me? I could've had you do something else, so you didn't have to deal with people".

"You need to come to work," she continued "You're already at risk of losing your job". Although she was right, how was I going to hide the big black eye I had? I didn't wear make-up, so that was not an option. I recently got some micro braids and tried my best to make a swoop over the eye that was messed up but that didn't work. Forget it! I needed my job so off I went. April was nice enough to keep me on the floor and turned the lights down so no one would be able to see my eye. It was a long night, but I managed to stay out of sight and hold my head down so my hair would fall in my face if I were approached. When six o'clock came, I was all but too happy to go home. Sadly, she was still tasked with letting me go. I knew this wasn't personal and that she was only doing her job.

After getting some rest, I decided I would clean the house and wash clothes to try and erase the horrific details of what happened the night before. My dad had been released and now lived in the boarding house a couple of streets over. He and I started meeting at the laundry mat on Fridays to catch up. Considering the "shiner" I had, I didn't really want to see him, so I didn't call. Just as I was about to leave, he called. He asked if I was coming out because he wanted a cigarette. He was in the process of quitting, so he would sometimes bum from me. Lying to him wasn't an option, so I told him I was on the way to the laundromat. "Oh, ok, I'll just walk down there," he replied. I hung up the phone, cursing to myself about what he would say. Daniel dropped us off as he didn't want to face my dad because of my sporty new look. As I put the clothes in the wash, my dad walked in. He spoke to the boys as they continued horseplaying throughout the laundromat. I made an attempt to hide my face by letting my braids down, so they would dangle. After I started the washer, we walked outside to smoke when he discovered what I was hiding. "Brandy," he said. "Da, I know so, please don't start," I replied. "No, you don't know," he said, "do you see yourself?" he asked. "Yes, I do," I replied disrespectfully, "but it was an accident," I concluded. "Honestly, I don't want to talk about it" I scolded. "Ok," he said, leaving it there. He finished his cigarette and asked for one more before he left. I could tell he couldn't handle the fact that his daughter was being abused, but he also knew I was old enough that there was nothing he could do.

Having him back was a blessing and a curse. I didn't understand the nuances of sobriety and what it took to maintain. While he was putting up a brave front, I could tell he was frustrated to see what had become of me. In an attempt to do things right and get his life together, he and Norma married. My siblings and I weren't invited, and it was held in Winston-Salem. Now that he was heavy in the church, our lives drifted, and we met less and less. While it was a blessing for them, I could only see the curse. Now his time was split between Norma, I, and the church with the two of them reigning supreme. Even my mom was jealous of his newfound love and constantly called when she was drunk to express her anger. This confused me since she was the one who left and filed for divorce. I guess in her mind he owed her this life and not Norma.

It was months looking for employment that paid enough to afford the bills. I was forced to apply for food stamps, even though after receiving one payment, I was investigated. When I reflect on that time, I sometimes say God didn't want me to have that life. Other times, I say Daniel must've been dating someone at DSS because it was too weird. Either way, they decided I was committing fraud and stopped my assistance. After trying work as a daycare teacher and a salesperson, I found work in the kitchen at a convenience store. My hours were 6am-2pm, so most days I drove except Fridays when Daniel got off early. Things weren't perfect but they were manageable until he came to pick me up but decided to leave me because I didn't come out on time. Now I could say that we had an argument but that was not the case. Somewhere in his demented mind he thought leaving me while it was pouring down raining was ok. I was so embarrassed that I walked out of the store as if he were waiting for me. As I walked down Darrien 16 in disbelief, I hoped this was a prank gone wrong. Just then a stranger pulled over and asked if I needed a ride. I gave the driver my dad's address instead of my own. Here I was in someone's van not knowing if they were a serial killer hoping God protected me enough to make it home. After that awful experience, I got a job at the McDonald's that was in walking distance of my house. Never again would I put myself in that type of predicament.

While I worked second shift at McDonald's, I continued to look for a better opportunity. Since I had dropped out of high school, I thought my opportunities were limited. Because I was a quick learner and hard worker, the managers always presented a leadership role, but I wasn't interested in growing in those establishments. Each week I got the latest career builder and there was always a need for school bus drivers. The pay was a lot more than I was making and the only qualification was six month driving experience. As soon as that time came for me, I applied. I received the call for orientation, and I knew this was my chance. But when I found out the class was a week, on N. Tryon, and wasn't on the bus route, I was devastated. How was I going to make this work? Daniel decided it was too much trouble for him to allow me to drive every day. Which was selfish since he didn't work that far from home, and his mom could have dropped him off. I did not allow this to stop me. My mom wasn't working, so I asked her if she could take me. She declined as well but did allow me to drive her car. It didn't matter as long as I made it. Every day I came home and studied because I was determined to pass.

Friday came, and it was time to test my knowledge. I took a last look at my notes to make sure I was ready. I was so nervous that I locked the keys in the car. Luckily a classmate offered to let me use her AAA. I could've kicked myself when the proctor announced it was open book if you had it. "What"! Oh well, I was on my own. It wasn't that hard but some of the test questions were tricky. After I gave my test to the proctor, he asked me to have a seat while he graded it. I was so happy when he called me back up to say, "You passed".

Although it was only 8:30 in the morning, I wanted someone to be as excited as I was. That was the first time I learned that everyone will not be happy for you like you want them to be. My brother and his girlfriend had gotten another apartment on the east side of town close to where I had taken my class. So eager to celebrate, I called to tell them the good news and that I was on the way. When I arrived, they were still in bed as if I had never called. It was a waste of my gas and time, so I stayed for a minute and left.

The proctors asked what side of town you lived on to assign you closest to your house. I was dispersed to the Wilkerson Blvd location for the driving portion of the exam. It was three days of me learning how to drive a bus when I was new to driving period. Still, I would not let this deter me, and at the end of the training, I passed with flying colors. People told me how important these licenses were and how they could make for a good career if I used them. All I knew was I needed a job, and now I had one. There was still a transportation issue because I was assigned to pick up my bus from North Tryon and be to work at 5 am. So, it was back to my mom asking for her assistance, and she allowed me to drive her car until Leroy began to complain. If I could just hold on until tax time, I could get me a car. Getting everyone else on board with that plan was going to be the biggest problem.

Since Leroy had gotten my mom the car, I was at his mercy. It was a daily struggle, but it was one I managed to overcome with pleading and begging. They, too, were upset that Daniel was unwilling to help me, especially once the liquor began to flow, but I shifted the focus. I didn't need the constant reminder of what I didn't have. I was just asking for help at this moment. This was one of the reasons I stayed in my situation; I wasn't allowed the grace to need help; it was always the requirement that I figure things out on my own. When the day came to file taxes, I did just that. Now, it was time to wait for my refund.

The route I'd taken over was meant to be precise on the pickup times because of the first stop being in Davidson. As a result, I was taken off that route and put on a route that I had to be there at 6 am. This was better for my transportation problems, even if my ego couldn't understand it. It was like moving from the suburbs back into the hood, so it was a hard pill to swallow. The day came when my tax check was ready, and so was I. It was straight to the car lot for me. Now, from my history of making payments, I knew I needed to pay for a car, but I didn't have time to look for one. I needed a car now.

Getting up that morning, I was filled with excitement. It was like waking up on Christmas morning, but only this time I was going to have something waiting for me that I had asked for. Santa may have been a disappointment, but Uncle Sam made up for some of that today. This was my first time at a car lot, so I was what the car salesman may refer to as good bait. Daniel had volunteered to accompany me, but I wanted to do this on my own. If I was ever going to become independent, I had to start separating my life to become comfortable with that way of living. I was on my break, so I hoped we could get this process done quickly so I could make it back to work on time. Unfortunately, car dealerships do not work on your time and continue to hold you there for no clear reason. Finally, I found the car I wanted.

In The Damn Way

It was a Mazda 6 with a leather interior and a stick shift. They helped me learn how to drive it, and I was all set. It was sporty, flashy, and sexy, all I thought I needed in a car. It was black with caramel-colored leather interior. It had a sunroof, AM/FM with a CD player, Bose speakers, tint, and sporty rims. There was nothing I would have to do to this car but get in and drive. I was smiling hard while waiting to get into my new car and return to work. I was ready to show off what I had to those who were rooting for me to fall behind my back. That wasn't who I was, and I was reminded of that when they came back and said, "You're going to need a cosigner". Either no one was willing or didn't have the credit to cosign. I called everyone, including my grandma, which was not easy for me to do, asking for help. Defeated, it was time for me to go back to work, but they told me they would continue working on it.

While at work, they called and said they had another car for me. They asked me if I could come back after I got off and take a look, and if I agreed, they would try to get me in this car. Although I was grateful, they kept their word, I was upset that I would no longer be able to stunt. I sulked the entire time I was driving, but I went back in hopes that what they had was just as good. It was a red, four-door, 2000 Mitsubishi Mirage. I didn't know too much about this car and wasn't impressed at all. There was something I didn't understand, which was why it was so important for me to stunt on people who were not intricate to my growth. What I was doing for myself, and my boys was amazing, but my focus was on much smaller things. This car was big enough and small enough for me and the boys. Once I realized my simple mindedness, I focused on what was right before my eyes, reality. The process was taking so long that Daniel brought the boys to wait with me. Having toddlers is hard enough, but it was almost impossible in this environment. I was so happy with what the wait was going to produce that I didn't let it bother me much. After many hours, the wait was over, and I had my first car.

Of course, the decision was made for the boys to ride home with me. It didn't matter because, for the first time I and my boys had something that belonged to us. We rode home blasting the music and singing to whatever was on the radio. I was screaming and thanking God for this wonderful blessing. As we sped down I-85, I pondered my next task: getting us a better place to live. So much had occurred since we moved here that I figured it was time for a fresh start now that I had a car. I looked in the apartment guide until I found the perfect fit. My mind had been conditioned to go to the local realtor, better known as slumlords, to get a list of apartments or houses that were likely infested with roaches. As I looked in the apartment guide, I saw apartment complexes that fit the same criteria but found one that was perfect. One day, after I got off my bus, I went over to talk with the management and get a tour of the apartments. Although it was still on the west side, it was far enough to make me feel like I was in a different part of town. As we walked through the neighborhood, she highlighted the amenities, and I fell in love with the place. When we arrived at the condo/apartment, I was amazed at how nice it was. It was a cute two-bedroom condo with carpet and washer/dryer connection. It had an open floor plan so I wouldn't feel so closed off if we were to have company. Also, a balcony that overlooked the back where we could cook on the grill. The parking lot was not easily accessible as it was separated by a large plot that housed trees and well-tended grass. Across the street was a public park where the boys could play since the park in the neighborhood was a bit small. They made up for it with the pool that I pictured us getting in once it was warm enough. I was sold, and we returned to the office to do the paperwork. The process would take a few days, so I didn't get my hopes up.

Meanwhile, it was back to business as usual, but now I was in control, and it felt good. Although I lost the premium route, they added afterschool, so I wasn't missing any money. This was good financially, but it meant I got home later, so Daniel was responsible for picking up the boys and feeding them. Some days he did good by ensuring they were fed, and bathed, which made the day a lot easier. As promised, I received a call about the apartment with an approval. OMG! My first real apartment, as I would consider it as if the one I was in was a trial apartment. When moving day came, I was overjoyed. We packed, but because we were young, dumb, and inexperienced, what we didn't have a box for, they put in trash bags. It was ghetto, but I didn't care. We were moving, and that was all I cared about. I stopped in to see how things were going on my way back to the bus parking. It's funny how much junk you accumulate when you move somewhere. It was a Friday night, and we were determined to make this a one-and-done. When I got home, we packed up the last of the last, and off we went to our new place. I was naïve to think that all our troubles were staying right there in that apartment on Haines Street, but it was in the car with us.

Of course, with something new and shiny, everything feels okay. It felt good coming home to a nice place, and the boys enjoyed having a park to go to. Company was not as frequent, so my weekends were sometimes filled with just the boys, me, and others as a family. Sometimes, my sister came over, and her, I and the boys would go to the pool. I couldn't swim well but hoped that I could teach them by taking them. They loved playing around but teaching them to swim was a flop. Daniel continued to go out on the weekends, but it didn't bother me as much as it used to. Before Kisha, Megan, and I followed them since all our men went out and cheated. Once I got my car and moved, it became redundant. Kisha wouldn't know when to stop but my thought was if they are going to do it they would.

Now that my dad was heavily in the church, the boys and I tried to join as much as possible. I hoped we could do this as a family, but it's hard when you stay out all night on Saturday to go to church on Sunday. Honestly, I don't think he would've gone if he had been home. Our family needed intervention if we wanted any chance of surviving together. Unfortunately, it was no concern of his, so I went in hopes of saving myself and the children. I loved watching my dad play the bass guitar in the church band. The joy on his face as he played was one, I longed to have. It was as if he was playing for God only as he bore a look of peace from giving God glory. Although the church was not very big, they always performed well.

Although my dad has his reservations about the black eye, he had grown a liking to Daniel as a person. In his mind, Daniel was a man who took care of his home, and he respected that. My dad was a very hard worker and cared for his wife, which was important to him. I allowed him to let that be his vision of the man I hoped Daniel to become. Although Daniel was not a monster, and he contributed to the home, he also contributed to the stress I endured by being with him, so I wasn't seeing the hero my father was making him out to be. The respect came in handy when Daniel lost his job for horseplaying at work and fell off the forklift. He wasn't seriously hurt, but enough for him to be out of work, receive workmen's compensation, and an investigation that led to his termination. In my mind, he was trying to be cute by wooing some girl, but he got messed up. His story stated that he and some others were horsing around, and he slipped in some water and fell. Either way the result was he no longer had a job. My dad was happy to help as the company he worked for was used to hiring illegal immigrants, so they were not perplexed by his felony. He was endorsing a person who was a hard worker and smart, so it wasn't a gamble they were taking by hiring him. It wasn't long before Daniel was promoted to be my father's supervisor. I didn't see it lasting long in my heart as Daniel constantly complained about the long hours he had to work. Honestly, I was happy as at least I knew he wasn't with another woman because none worked there except for the receptionist, and she was married and older.

Scared that Daniel's income would be requested, or I would be responsible for paying for daycare, I didn't turn in my paperwork to Childcare Resources. This was a selfish move since I didn't have a backup plan. While I attempted to beat the system, I was the one being beat. After probably a lot of persuasion on my dad's behalf, Norma finally agreed to babysit, but there was a fee. At first, I was livid as she didn't work, but I had to understand that she was not my mom, and these were not her grandchildren. It didn't relieve my sense of entitlement that I felt from my parents that since they didn't raise me, they should've done everything for free. Since my dad's house was on my way to work, I dropped them off, and Daniel picked them up. Every morning, she had breakfast waiting for them, and when Daniel picked them up, they were fed. All that was left was a bath before they were put to bed. I don't know if I ever told her, but I was grateful for her time with the boys. Not only that, but she made sure there was enough breakfast for me before I went to work. Things were working well.

We were not used to having company unless it was someone coming to get their hair done or Daniel's brother to play the game. Typically, he met his friends at his mom's house, and they went from there. So, I was excited when Daniel was on board that Ben and Missy were coming over for spades and drinks. I didn't expect Missy to invite her girlfriend to accompany them. Her name was Tish, and I didn't know much about her. She was about 5'10, brown skinned and full-figured. Her hair was long and was in a nice roller set. I certainly didn't trust her. At first, I tried my best to be a great host, but the more drinks I poured, the less she was welcome in my home. Through my jaded eyes of every woman, I saw her flirting with him. I was drunk, but I could tell she was looking for her next beau and I was ready to let her know I don't play them games. She apologized, but it was too late. I was already upset and, so she decided to leave. Women in her predicament were always looking for their next meal ticket, and unless I said take him, it was not going to be my man. She was a single mom who thought she was better than any woman because she was pretty and her version of thick. From the random gossip sessions I had with Missy, I knew she was used to whoring her way to someone else's man, which was why I was confused as to why she brought her. That night, she found out that I was not the one. Unfortunately, she had ridden with my brother, so they had to leave as well. It became the first and last time I saw her. It wasn't just her that I lit into that night. Daniel was not innocent, and I let him know as well. You don't know me like that.

A few months later, we decided to host another card night. This time, I made sure to tell Missy to leave her friends at home. Everything was going well until Daniel's brother called, and they planned to go out. Daniel assured me that he was not going, so don't get upset. It didn't look like his brother understood that he wasn't going because he kept calling, asking where he was. Not long after his brother and some friends pulled up because Daniel was not. Daniel pulled me aside and said, "Let me get $20". "20 dollars?" I replied. "I thought you weren't going," I asked. "I'm not. I'm just going to pretend like I'm going," he said. "What the hell? Just tell him you're not going", I responded. "Just give me the money", he said, so I replied, "If you leave, I'm leaving". It was the first time I stood my ground as leaving and meant every word I said. Although his response was, "man, you better sit your ass down, I'll be right back," I still responded, "I'm telling you right now, if you leave, I'm leaving," as I looked him square in his eyes. History had taught him that he was in control, but what he didn't understand was that I was growing up and becoming my own woman. He had control over the little girl who didn't have a father in me, not the woman who was getting up making her own way. I watched him walk down the steps as we lived on the second floor, get in his car, and leave. "Ok" I said to myself and told Jeffery and Missy "let's go". The boys were asleep, so after I refreshed myself, I put their coats on, and off we went.

A huge part of me hoped he would turn the corner and come back, but I knew him enough to know that would not be the case. Instead, we decided to take the boys to their house with Missy's teenage daughter and son. As I sat in the back with the boys, I did my best to reassure them that everything was ok. My heart was tired of being broken, and I was tired of dragging my boys through the mess that their father. This was my opportunity to leave without the headache of arguing and fighting, but something kept me from making that decision. *As I flashed back to months prior, I remembered Daniel putting the fear of God in me with a gun, so I knew what he was capable of. He still worried about the lie that was told about Jim, and he thought he could scare me into telling the truth. I was used to the way he treated me, but now he was bringing our children into this. Although I cried, saying it was a lie, he pulled out that silver 45 told me to open my mouth, and with all the anger you could have for a person, said, "I'll kill you". It was the first and only time that he had ever done this, but the effects were unfathomable. To hear your children screaming and you not knowing what to do for fear that he might be crazy enough to use this gun changes your focus. Although he eventually retreated, I took my children, and we left. We had nowhere to go, so we stayed in the car until he and the boys fell asleep.* As I shook my head, attempting to erase the memory, I came back to us, pulling up to their house. Reluctantly, I kissed the boys and reassured them that I would be back. I would have rather gone home and forgotten that this day happened, but I felt I needed to prove a point. You become drained and complacent after you have endured so much from a person. You try your best to live in peace while putting your feelings and emotions on hold. You convince yourself that the good times made up of family outings to the park, a few laughs over a stupid joke, or the last-minute gift you received on Valentines make up for it all. Finally, you decide that they will change if I stand up and let my voice be heard. There's an issue with that voice. It's no longer yours. Everything you say and do keeps them in your life until you decide that you love yourself more and this person no longer deserves your love. Unfortunately, I wasn't at that point, but I was at the point of being petty. Here I was, 20 years old, not able to buy alcohol, but on her way to party with real adults.

Ben partied for a while now, so he was familiar with all the hot spots. The issue was finding a place that would allow me in without asking me for an ID. Not only was I not old enough, I looked younger than I was. We pulled up to this house that, from the outside, was nothing you would expect from a liquor house. The ones I had visited before and since have given me the impression that I needed to watch my back because someone might stab me. That sounds ignorant as I say it out loud but compared to Ben my life was really sheltered in what I knew about the world. I had experienced liquor houses, but they were older homes or apartments where they had regulars who were probably there day in and out. Some had the ladies of the night and dealers making their money while they sipped on a limited bar filled with Seagram's Gin, Canadian Mist, Schlitz Malt liquor, and Budweiser beer. This home was nicely maintained. It was green with motion lights all around. You could faintly hear the music, which kept it hidden from the law. As we finally found somewhere to park, Ben gave me a speech about staying quiet and letting him do all the talking. He knew I had been drinking already, and when I'm drinking, my mouth gets even looser. We walked up the steps, and Ben shook hands with a man whom I would describe as the bouncer. As they were talking, the door opened, and this place was not any liquor house. This was a club, and everyone was in there having a good time. This made me more excited, and I started grooving to the song playing. The bouncer started to allow us to go in before he stopped me and said, "I need your ID". Uh oh, this was not in the plan, but I replied, "I don't have it". Ben quickly jumped in and added, "That's my sister". The bouncer was cool as he stated, "ok, but if she doesn't have an ID, she cannot come in". Dang!

He tried everything, but he wasn't having it. As we were leaving, we ran into one of the many people Ben knew, John. John had been around the family for a while, so I knew of him. He wasn't as old as Ben but old enough to get into the place. When Ben explained that we were going somewhere else because of my ID, John decided he would ride with us. It was the first time I understood that being the new girl always meant someone was going to try to play you.

He was a nice-looking, brown-skinned, 5'7 guy with a nice smile, so when he started spitting game, I entertained for the moment. Although I knew he had a girlfriend, I selfishly talked him up to make him believe he had a chance. As we arrived at our next destination, he still talked about going home with me. The buzz I had from the alcohol we drank at my house was wearing off, so he was beginning to get on my nerves. We got out of the car at the next after-hours spot that was nothing like the one we were at before. It was a place much like the ones I had experienced before, but I did my best to enjoy myself. The house was a small "shotgun" house, where you could be at the front and see straight through the back door. There was no security guard, and everyone looked like they had been "rolled hard and put away wet," as Funky Dineva says. That just means they were regulars and probably had been there since the place opened. They had cups in their hands that they were barely drinking from because they were already drunk. It was a sight to see as Ben walked through the place as he was regarded as a superstar. The men gave him dap, and the women gave him hugs as they asked where he had been. Missy and I walked behind him and let him receive all the glory he deserved. They knew her, but he reassured her by reminding the women that she was his woman. As he introduced me, it gave me a more comfortable feeling about a place where you had to be ready for whatever was liable to happen.

To my surprise, the place was very clean, and although you knew that there were drug dealers and users, pimps, and prostitutes, and johns looking for a good time, everyone was very cordial. If any transactions were being made, they were done in a respectful way. As we moved towards the kitchen, we saw where the action really was. Men were sitting at the table smoking cigarettes and cigars as they gambled playing cards. To the left was the numbers man handing out tickets to those paying to hopefully win a few hundred once the number was pulled. He stood next to the owner of the house, who was also the bartender. This was where I wanted to be in the middle of the action. My reality started to creep back into my brain, and the consequences of my going home were troubling. I hoped he was still gone, and that I could sneak back in as if nothing happened. Ben got us some drinks and I stood there sipping, trying to be as social as possible. The one thing about being the new person is they feel you out before engaging with you, and I was not fitting into their comfort level. It didn't bother me much as I was trying to gain courage from drinking, so they were not as important to me. After about an hour, Ben asked if I was ready to go, and I was. We took John back to his car, and when he went inside to let whoever know he was going with us, we left. Even if Daniel and I broke up, I wasn't about to trade in one cheater for another.

Although we were only 15 minutes away from my house, the thoughts going through my mind made the ride that much longer. Because we lived at the top of the hill, you could see who was parked at our house as you turned into the complex. There it was, Daniel's white Nissan 200 nicely parked in the parking lot. Immediately, I told him to leave before he saw us. Although he was probably in the house, I wasn't taking any chances. Jeffery asked "why" as he was not privy to the many fights Daniel and I had prior to this night. Even if he had been, he was unaware that it was enough to make me fearful of going home, which upset him. It was the first time I had admitted my true feelings about this relationship, and I was embarrassed as I responded, "I don't feel like fighting tonight". The music was loud in the car as I had added woofers and a new stereo system with an amp. No one said anything as we drove to their house. The view of my life had just become real to Jeffery and me when I admitted to myself that I was afraid of Daniel. When I told people about this years later, they had no idea because we always showed up as The Couple, but we were far from it. That's not to say things were always bad, but there were surely some trying times.

The next day, I was awakened by a booming system outside, and I knew exactly who it was: Daniel. Being that I was hungover, this was the last thing I wanted to deal with. I looked at my cell phone and realized he had called several times. He had never been to my brother's house, so he didn't know which apartment it was until he saw my car parked outside the house. My first instinct was to let him drive around clueless, but I knew that would only make things worse. We had played enough games for one night it was time to face the music. Sleeping on their couch was miserable and I severely wanted my bed, but it was time I stood for something. I locked the screen door and spoke to him through the door. "Let's go," he said. "No," I replied, "I'm not going with you". He pulled on the screen door with no success. "Brandy, I'm not playing with you," he stated. "Neither am I", I replied. "Ok," he stated with a voice of revenge. In my mind, I was gone and never going back. In my heart, I knew the fear of the unknown would set in, but I was willing to try anyway. My boys deserved more, even if I thought I didn't, so it was time I made a choice. Although he got in his car and pulled off, a part of me didn't feel like he left. Daniel had shown me he needed control, and the mere fact that I had taken that away from him made me unable to see him backing down that easily. He continued to call, trying to convenience me to come home. He stated he wasn't going to do anything, but I wasn't going for it. We stayed in the house just in case he came back. I did my best not to discuss anything in front of the boys and cautiously walked outside to talk to him when he called. Sunday morning, I went to Walmart to get the boys and me some change of clothes as I had to go back to work, and we could all use a bath. Although I badly wanted to go home, I had a point to prove, and I was going to see it through.

Monday morning came with a buzzer-beater, the minutes dwindling as I attempted to hash out my escape plan. Ben and Missy welcomed us into their home with open arms and no expiration date, but the house began to fill to the brim. Their children had gotten older, and as friends and romantic partners funneled through the house, it became an environment I didn't want for my boys. The events from the weekend ran circles in my head, much like my bus routes. Although I could see the destination, the roads continued to wind. As I pulled up to the house, my anxiety intensified as I tried to imagine what he had done while I was gone. Although I knew he was at work, it didn't help me as I struggled to calm myself down. I had traveled to several parking lots within the complex to confirm that he was not hiding his car. I was taken aback with what I witnessed as I entered the house.

This was the first time I saw Daniel's emotions about losing his family unfortunately, I felt like it was too little too late. There were beer bottles straggled around the living room that indicated someone had joined him or he had drowned himself in alcohol. It was the holiday, so we put up a Christmas tree that was no long in its place, only a trail of ornaments, so I gathered that he had thrown it away. On the floor, in pieces, lay my salon pro hair dryer, which I used to make extra money. All I could think about was this could have been me that he released this anger upon. Material items can be replaced, so what he took away was insignificant to my peace. With that in mind, I stopped looking at what was lost and began searching for what I came for. The boys and I needed our clothes, and I needed my uniforms for work. As I went to my dresser to look for my things, I quickly noticed something peculiar. Everything was missing! I checked the dirty laundry and the washer and dryer just in case I had forgotten them, but there was nothing. I had underestimated how much attention he paid to me and what was going on in my life. He knew it was mandatory that I wore my uniform and made sure I would have to call him if I wanted them. Reluctantly, I picked up the cordless phone on the kitchen wall and called Daniel to locate my things.

"Hey, where is all of my stuff?", I asked "What stuff?" he answered. "My clothes, underwear, uniforms, they are all missing," I stated "They in there" he said. "In where," I asked, "I have looked everywhere, and I don't see anything." As I was speaking, suddenly it became quiet in his background. Daniel worked in a warehouse, and any time I called him, you could hear the noise of the nail gun pounding the wood or other forklifts in the background. As soon as I noticed the change, I began moving towards my car. "Why did you leave and not come home?" he continued to ask. "You left, and I told you not to leave," I answered. He couldn't fathom that just because he expected something from me, it cleared him from living up to the same expectation. This was a relationship of 50/50, or at least that's what I told myself, and I'm certain he thought it was 70/30. I saw him pulling up just as I expected, but I didn't fret as I had already locked myself inside my car. Immediately, he jumped out of his car demanding for me to get out. "No!" I responded. If he wanted to speak to me, he was going to have to calm down. I wasn't completely powerless, and today, I was going to make sure he understood that. "Brandy, I will bust this window," he said, "Go ahead," I taunted. Finally, he calmed down and asked if we could talk. I said, "We're talking now". Fumbling over his words he attempted to make me understand his side of why he went with his brother. This conversation was not moving in the direction he'd hoped for and his phone rang constantly. He was supposed to be at work, but they noticed he was gone, so he didn't have much time. "Can we talk as a family?" he asked. At first, I was reluctant, but a part of me saw the sincerity of what it meant for him to have his family and said, "Ok". What a fool? I was out, gone, safe, and here I was, going back to the lion's den. I also wanted my family, so I was willing to give it another chance. Before he left, he told me my things were in the kitchen cabinets.

As I walked back towards the house, I tried to understand how he fit my clothes into the kitchen cabinets. We only had two full cabinets cramped for space, but the other cabinets were half that size. I was able to recover some of my things from the cabinet, and I concluded that he had thrown the others away. In addition, I was left with only one work uniform shirt as he cut up the others. Out of all our arguments, this was the only one where he allowed his rage to pour out in this way. Because he had made this mess it was only right that he cleaned it, so I got my one good shirt and went to my mom's until it was time for work. I decided against telling her about the intricate details of the weekend as I knew what her response would be: leave. While that thought never left, I didn't need anyone to tell me what I already knew. Especially someone who also suffocated my mind, heart, and soul with the endless tyranny from her traumatic childhood. As I lay on the couch, I replayed the conversation repeatedly, hoping that what I had agreed to was not another trap.

Work was a blur while I attempted to come up with answers to the anticipated questions from Daniel. In my response, I wanted to make sure that he understood that I no longer wanted to live with him in an abusive environment. Unfortunately, getting Daniel to listen and hear you could be impossible, so I tried to be prepared.

By the time I picked up the boys, I was no more convinced I'd made the right decision to come back than I was that morning. There were a lot of what ifs that made this harder to suffer if they were unveiled. As I pulled up to the condo, I took a deep breath and hoped for the best. I turned to the boys with a smile of safety that I would protect them. Their response was a look of the same. They were my only concern. We walked into an embracement that I had never received from Daniel for as long as we had been together. He had cleaned up and attempted to assemble the broken items. As I looked at my dryer, all duck taped, I thought to myself that dryer was an exact replica of what I thought of myself. All broken and being held together by some duct tape, but only I could see my cracks. No one else could imagine the pain I held inside but God. As the conversation continued from earlier, it revealed no new details than before. He gave no plausible reasoning for what he had done but made sure to yield sympathy by telling me how us leaving home had hurt him. Unfortunately, he was the only one who could confirm or deny if he was lying about that. During the conversation, he said something that struck me as odd "We should get married. You're not going anywhere, and neither am I, so it makes sense."

Wow! He wanted to marry me because we were not going anywhere. As I sat there on our black leather couch looking at him, I remembered the times I fought females because they spoke about wanting him. Also, I recalled the gruesome arguments that almost always ended in physical altercations that always left emotional scars. It was hard not to look at him and scream "Hell No" when I look back on the fear I saw in my children's eyes as I did my best to protect myself and them. Slowly, I turned to him and gave him the only answer that felt right for this question...

{ 9 }

For Better?

"Yes?", what was I thinking? In six years, this man had shown me what he was capable of, and now I was going to forget all of that and become his wife. Finally, I was going to give my children the one thing that had been taken from me: a real home. A home that consisted of their mom and father, no matter how unhappy it made everyone. If I could pretend, I had been happy for the last ten years, I could teach my children how to do the same. Nowhere in my mind did I think what I was doing to them wasn't healthy for their growth. No sooner than I answered his question, I was ready to call everyone and tell them the exciting news. We called his family first and everyone was already excited as his sister had just announced that she was marrying Jim. Neither one of them deserved us, but we were both ready to serve them on a platinum platter. The response from my family was not embraced with the same open arms. Unfortunately, they had seen the damage this relationship had already borne upon my life but were willing to support me if I was happy. So that was it: we were going to get married, and no one was willing to step up and tell us that this was a bad idea. The date was set for February 16, 2002, and I was full speed ahead, making this day the best day ever.

Typically, the bride's parents pay for the wedding but that was not going to be the case. This was not going to be the fairytale that most girls dream, but if I wanted to make something happen, I would be responsible for payments. Although my dad was rehabilitated from drugs, his financial literacy was never seen fit to be, and so whatever money he made was overextended by his mismanaging of money. My mom was no longer working, so her sole income was laid at Leroy's feet. This left only me, as now that Daniel had what he wanted, he washed his hands with it all. Luckily, my mom was friends with someone who could help; her name was Carol. Carol was a longtime daycare and club owner in the old neighborhood. Carol was about 6 feet, brown-skinned with broad shoulders. She talked loudly and was ready to back it up at any cost. People respected her more than they feared her, making her into the businesswoman she was. Camila had gone to her daycare, and when my mom was late, and the responsibility fell on me to pick up Camila, Carol fussed but was always understanding. Although I wasn't a huge fan of some of the words that came from her mouth, I could put my feelings aside to get this wedding done. She had done her daughter's wedding, and everything was beautiful, so I was confident with her being my wedding planner.

Although Carol was strong with her instructions, the opposition from those receiving those instructions was a lot stronger. I had chosen 12 of my closest family members to represent me on my special day, and the majority were making sure it wasn't as special as I hoped. After work or during my break I spent most of my time making sure they were where they needed to be as well as doing what I needed for me. We only had three months to complete everything. My maid of honor was Camila and because of school, was limited to what she could do. Besides she was 16 and knew no more about this than I did. Thankfully, tax time was near because I was digging into my bill money, which was creating more of a problem. The stress of it all mounted with each passing day, but I did my best to keep my head up. This was on top of the arguments Daniel and I were continuing to have over this and that, which foolishly, I thought were gone when I said yes. It took everything I had to show up for work and keep a smile on my face when I wanted to quit, move, and be done with everyone.

In The Damn Way

Two weeks away from becoming husband and wife, I decided to go by his parents' house. His brother had come over and I didn't want to sit with the two of them. It was anything unusual, as I usually went there when Daniel had company. This night, his dad decided to plant the seed I was stealing from his mom. Not in such a way that was evident but in a way that I was the joke of the room. When I was able to understand that the joke was about me, it infuriated me, so I grabbed the boys and left. Here, I was running from one fake family to enter another. I always assumed they talked about me, but I hoped that it was my insecurities and not reality. Immediately, I went home and called off the wedding. No way was I going to marry someone whose family felt I was capable of stealing money. This defamation of my character hurt more because I was the one everyone was willing to trust. Daniel was angered by the lies and the fact that I no longer wanted to be his wife. Immediately he left to confront his dad and put a stop to this. Later, I found out he never confronted his dad because his sister stopped him and expressed how he "knew how his dad was". When he came home, we talked about everything and decided to proceed with the wedding. His dad never apologized and only said, "you know how family is" to cover up what he'd done. Although he was always the one you had to watch for somehow, I thought I was exempt from that.

As I woke up that Friday, I replayed the last couple of months and how much stress it had caused. Finally, all the girls had taken their fabric for the bridesmaid's dresses we were having custom-made. Our colors were burgundy, cream, and black, so their shoes had to be dyed burgundy to match the dresses and shawls. Thankfully everyone had gotten it done after 1000 times of being told. My mom complained because I bought her and Daniel's mom the same dress, so no one felt left out. You would have thought she would be grateful since I paid for the dresses. She also requested I allow Leroy to walk me down the aisle. If my dad was deceased maybe but that was not an option. He and I had grown to be cordial, but he understood how I felt. Daniel's guys were just as stressful as Ben waited until we got to the store to say he didn't have the money to get his tux. This meant I had pick up the cost so that he didn't look like a total clown. Lately this had become our relationship. Me picking up the pieces where he decided to leave them. If we could get through this last day, everything would be over and done. Carol let me borrow her dress to save some money, but I was responsible for taking it to the cleaners. This was a reasonable choice because I didn't have any daughters and no real plans to have more children. It was an off-white princess wedding dress with a long train. The veil almost swallowed me with the amount of fabric and my issue of only being 5'2".

Everything was ready and all I had to do was get my hair done, go to rehearsal, and attend my bridal party. My hairdresser had agreed to do his sister's hair, and our appointment was set for 11. Daniel and I were to meet so we could get the marriage license when I was done. I didn't want to have to come all the way back to get her, so I decided to wait. It was taking forever, and Daniel was angrily calling and calling. As soon as she was done, I hit the gas, trying to get there as soon as we could. Unfortunately, by the time we reached the office, they were closed. What we didn't know what that they closed early on Friday. Daniel was upset, and I could understand to some degree. I was more afraid than disappointed to be honest. The last thing I wanted was to have to cancel everything that everyone had been hassled and some worked so hard to make happen. When I told Carol what happened, she suggested we show up for rehearsal to see if he would marry us and let us bring the certificates on Monday.

As we arrived separately at the church, Carol was already there setting things up, and I could see that it was going to be beautiful. We met the pastor in his office and explained the situation, but he declined to marry us as it was "against the law". Carol was doing her best to remedy the problem but knew the likelihood of us getting married the next day was slim. Reluctantly, it was time we told every-one that tonight was canceled and that further instructions would be given as we received it. Carol decided to break the bad news since she was the wedding planner. As she was talking, Daniel became enraged and turned to me and said, "You're a stupid bitch." Wow! Right on the church steps stood the man who had asked me to be his wife declaring that I wasn't worthy. I understand being upset, but this is how you handle your anger. My suspicions that he hadn't changed were verified that night. We left and as I reflected the part, I played I also questioned my decision.

We arrived back at his parents to figure out what was next. He continued to try and ruin my night, but my girls were not about to let that happen. Some of the girls, along with my coworkers, were planning a night I wouldn't forget, and I was ready. They were finally ready for me, so I left him standing at his mom's, lying about having a stripper party in the hotel room. Little did I know that's exactly what they had planned for me, and I enjoyed every moment of being free and not ridiculed. When I got home, he apologized again and decided we should take Carol's advice and see if the license office was open on Saturday. Unfortunately, they were not open, so we were going to have to reschedule. My preacher was unavailable, so we had to find another church to get married. Later I recognized how many red doors were slammed in my face telling me not to go through with this, but I didn't listen.

Monday morning, we were both off work, so we went, and successfully, we were able to obtain our marriage license. As I looked at them, everything became real. Through my life, if someone told me this would be the way I was proposed to and about to be married I would have laughed in their face. Carol was able to secure us another church, ironically, it was the church that her late husband and she had gotten married. From what I heard, he was Daniel times 10, leading to his demise, which was probably an omen. Although it was not the church, nor was he the preacher I wanted, we desperately said ok to be married across the street from where his mom and dad lived. Cummings Ave was known for obtaining a lot of things, but I don't think I had ever thought someone would be there to get married. The morning of the wedding, I was still running, which threw me behind, and my soon-to-be husband did everything to let me know it was on me. I finally reached the church to have my makeup done and get dressed. On the way, I was so angry and thought I shouldn't even show up, but I let go of that thought. As I watched everyone get ready while I was getting my makeup done, I was happy that this was almost over. Everyone looked so beautiful as we lined up to go into the church. It was a crisp winter day but sunny, which was helpful as the girl's dresses were sleeveless with a shawl. Kenya and Brooke helped with my dress while I smoked a cigarette to help me calm down. When we reached the door of the church, my stomach dropped. I had chosen "Here and Now" by Luther Vandross as my wedding march. As soon as the doors swung open and the songstress began to sing, a copious number of tears instantly fell from my eyes. So much so that my dad thought I was laughing. My makeup was ruined, but I made it down the aisle to become Mrs. Alexander. Sometimes, I wonder why I cried so hard but could never give a clear answer. We had a wonderful time, and for the first time in a long time, I felt like he loved me. It was February 23, 2002, and I felt like I had some "respect on my name" for the first time. Someone said that we should go to church together the next morning after getting married but that didn't happen.

{ 10 }

For Worse?

As I continue to grow, I understand more about a union and a partnership; honestly, I feel neither has anything to do with marriage. A union has a group of people together who make and assert the rules of an organization. A partnership is an agreement that both parties obtain equal ownership of a company. Neither one of them has the word love nor requires love for another person in the definitions but rather a liking for the cause put before them. It's only when you add God to either one of these that it becomes the institution of marriage. Society and organized religion have made us believe that without marriage, we are living wrong, but what about being married and despising one another.

With our home lives, we should've never entered a marriage without some counseling first or honestly at all. Love of God and with God was supposed to be at the center of all of it, but what had Daniel or anyone else at that time done to make me believe that I was loved or that I loved at all. Because of the wedding, my finances were out of control. I skipped one of my car payments trying to make our day beautiful, but it turned into a snowball effect. The more I tried to keep up, the more I fell behind, especially when the summer came. They were able to help me with a summer job, but it paid a lot less than what I was making, and by the time I received my paycheck I was behind another payment. Not only that, but it ended two weeks before school started, so it was another month before I received another paycheck. This made me three car payments behind with no way to catch up. It wasn't long before the take back man was following me, and I woke up to my car being repossessed. Because we were only married on paper and living as two individuals in a partnership, Daniel did nothing to help me save what was mine.

Thankfully, Daniel had two cars now that he had purchased a yellow 1981 Cadillac Sedan DeVille, which he began driving so that I could get to work. He didn't enjoy letting me drive his car any more than I enjoyed doing so. I remembered when he first got the Cadillac, and I took it one morning when the boys and I went to church. I chuckled when I saw him flying down Beatties Ford in my car, looking for me. For now, this was going to be the case until I could afford another car. To decrease expenses, I decided we should move to a cheaper place. My cousin lived in some apartments not far from where we lived and, in the daytime, it looked like a decent place to live. She had given them her thumbs up, and the price point was just what we needed to save a little money. I didn't know this was the hood and not the place for me and my family. As soon as we moved in, my cousin was moving out, and I began to question was this place what she told me it was. It was a two-bedroom townhome with 1 ½ bathrooms. Everything was a lot bigger compared to our previous apartment, and I didn't have to walk what seemed to be a mile from the parking lot to the door, which was a plus. There were only three apartments on my row, and the middle one was empty, so I didn't have to worry about someone making a lot of noise next door. There was a pool and a place for the kids to play, but I wouldn't call it a playground. I figured since we were close to the rent office at the front of the neighborhood, it would keep the brunt of whatever was going on where it was. For a while, everything was so good that my dad and his wife decided to move there.

In the fall of 2002 Daniel decided to play semi-pro football, so by the time we got home, it was shower, eat, and bed. During one of the games, Daniels cleats messed up and had to get a replacement pair at the nearest place, Kmart. These did not give him the support he needed, and, on a fabulous play, he was running for a touchdown, struck by a player, and tore a ligament in his ankle. This was detrimental as he would need surgery, and we could not make it on my income alone, nor did he have any insurance. Reluctantly, I called my insurance to add him, although this would mean more money coming from my check. Unfortunately, while they would add him, they would not pay for the surgery, so it was pointless. After the surgery, they said he would be out of work for six weeks. It was during this time some hard decisions had to be made. D was in HeadStart, but I was paying my mom to watch Davion, and this was going to have to stop if Daniel was going to be out of work. Davion was a quiet child who stayed to himself, and I knew he wasn't the type to be mischievous and get into things. Against Daniel's wishes, I told him Davion would have to stay with him while I ran my route. So, the mornings before I went to work, I put the TV on in their room, gave him his toys, told him not to move, and prayed nothing happened. When I came home, he was always where I left him, and I cooked us breakfast, tend to Daniel, make them lunch, put Davion back in the room in front of the TV with his toys, and went back to work. It wasn't one of my finest moments as a mom, but it was necessary at the time.

Daniel, being home with no control over his own life, was creating a multitude of problems. He was struggling with depression that was showing itself as anger, which was problematic. With Davion being home with him, I was afraid he would unknowingly take it out on him. Also, he was beginning to see what happens when we went to work and brewing up ideas. He was used to keeping things from me, so when we talked, he never expressed what he was experiencing, although I could tell something was wrong. When his job offered him light duty, I thought this would help clear some of the negative undertones that were filling our home. What I know now that I didn't understand at the time is when depression sneaks in it must be dealt with or it continues to feaster. This was the least amount of work Daniel, and I were responsible for in our lives, and yet it was bringing him even more discord than before. He was spending more time calling me because there was not much to do, and it was starting to aggravate me. Not that I didn't enjoy an occasional call, but it was like I had three children now because nothing was satisfying to him, and he spent the conversation complaining. I hoped his ankle would heal soon and he would go back to driving the forklift or find another job that brought him the purpose he was searching for. I didn't know that the Daniel I feared would truly appear was finally ready to show himself.

One January morning, after my bus route, I picked up Megan as I went to run some errands. At the time, she was the only one I trusted to be around. Although she was a common denominator between me and the family, I gave her the benefit of the doubt more than anyone else. It was tax season, so I was out buying some things for the house and paying bills when I received a call I wished never came. "Come and pick me up. I'm done with this job" he said. "What" I replied. "I'm tired of working here. Come and pick me up now," he said. Oh boy, I thought, this cannot be good. It was 10 a.m. and he had just gotten to work two hours before, so what could have happened that caused this drastic decision without consulting me. On the way there, I knew this was bad, but not only was I driving his car, but he was an adult, and if he wanted to quit, there was nothing more I could say. He was already at the edge of the street when I arrived, so I thought the job must have done something to him, but it was the exact opposite. He got in the car and started going on and on about how they got him messed up although they were the ones who were kind enough to allow him to work while he was healing. He didn't have a clear plan on what he would do now that he didn't have a job, or at least he didn't tell me. However, I could see his gears turning, and I knew that I would have to wait for it to unfold in order to understand what that meant.

When I dropped him off, there was a knot in the pit of my stomach. Most importantly, he was driving on crutches, which was not safe, but also because whatever he was planning was not good, it never was. A week later, I understood why he had kept his plans from me. I came home and there was a party going on, and I was not invited. Daniel had filed and received the tax refund and had chosen to buy some 22" chrome rims for his Cadillac. Not only that, he added subwoofers and now was looking like the rest of the dope boys. Guys from the neighborhood were suddenly close to Daniel and were hanging around his car and out in front of the house, which was unusual. When Daniel walked around to the back of the car where I stood, my first question was, "What's going on here?". "What do you mean?" he replied with a smirk, "we're just chillin". "Chillin, since when did you start chillin with the neighborhood?" I asked. "Look, while I was at home, I saw a lot of money being made," he began. "I'm tired of working hard and getting nowhere, and I've seen how things work and know I can do better". What the hell was he talking about? I thought this foolish talk was done when he was arrested less than ten years ago for thinking the same crap. Now, here we were, married with two children, and this clown thought it was time to start dealing again. The medicine he was taking must've been affecting his brain cells to think this was the way. Serious as I had ever been in my life, I turned to him and stated, "if you start selling drugs, I am going to take my children, and I'm leaving". "It's only weed," he said, "that's only a misdemeanor". Unfortunately, I had learned that Daniel was the worst liar, so I reassured him of my decision. "I'm not playing with you. I'm not about to put our children in this mess, so if you are about sell anything but weed, just know I'm taking our kids, and I'm leaving."

Honestly, I shouldn't have given him that much choice, but I was trying to hold on to the little piece left of us being a family. Growing up without one, I didn't want to lose this one, but I could see that no matter what, this man would be selfish. It was like looking through the looking glass and seeing my childhood replay itself. No matter what, I was not going to walk away from my job as a mom to my children, and if that meant doing it alone, I was going to prepare myself for that. Daniel started staying out late and sleeping all day, and I knew something else was going on. People who smoke weed are not looking for it all night. I knew that from experience. Davion was back home since I was the only one working, and again, I was responsible for making sure he was settled and fed before work. Most days, when I got off work, I'd take the boys and sit over my dad's just to get in the right frame of mind at home. Someone was always there and get was getting on my last nerve. We were back to arguing about what was really taking place. So much so that I was making stops on my way to pick up my afterschool children, which created more arguments. It was time to plan my escape because he had dug his heels into what he was going to do.

To make matters worse, somehow, KiKi found out that I drove a bus and decided she would stalk me at work. If I could catch this girl and whoop her butt, then maybe she would understand I'm not playing with her about this man. She could actually have him at this point if she could get him to leave. As I sat at a stop sign on my route, I noticed her pass by. I rolled my eyes because I couldn't follow her on the bus, and I really want to. Instead of going about her day, she played chicken with me while going downhill with children on my bus. She slowed down and would stop suddenly, hoping I would hit her. She knew that trying to stop a bus with hydraulic brakes going downhill was not as easy as a car. Thankfully, I was able to keep from hitting her, but she followed up by going to my job and telling them that I tried to hit her. I pleaded my case, but her mom was also a driver who was close with my supervisor, so it didn't end well. Unfortunately, I was suspended for three days but allowed to ride along to avoid losing money. If that wasn't enough, I missed my period. It was like I couldn't catch a break from the barrage of mess that continued to follow me.

After Davion I was responsible and received the Norplant which lasted years. I didn't want any accidents and since this would last for years, I felt it was the safest route. Unfortunately, it began giving me uncontrollable headaches, so I had it removed after three years. Reluctantly, they replaced it with the pill, which was not a good idea for me mentally but physically was the best because it didn't have as much progesterone. As I looked at that pregnancy test, my heart sank.

How could I be so reckless to allow something like this to happen? It was funny that a coworker of mine would periodically ask me if I was pregnant, and this time she didn't know. Daniel was not overjoyed but he was opposed to me having an abortion, which was my decision in the beginning. There was no way we needed to bring a baby into the mess we had created. Although I would have preferred to keep this to myself, I was forced to discuss it with my manager in order to get the day off. Stephanie was her name, and as long as I worked with her, she was always kind to me. She stopped me when I got to the next school and asked if she could pray with me. What she didn't and couldn't have known was everything Daniel and I had gone through. She could never understand why I felt what I felt. She only spoke to me from a religious point of view, and I respected her for that. Respectfully, I already had my mind made up and was unwilling to change.

The ride to the abortion clinic was as long as it was silent. Although it only took twenty minutes to get there, it felt longer because Daniel and I had nothing to say to one another. I don't know what I was expecting, but whatever it was the clinic was not that. Girls and women of all ages and ethnicities filled the clinic. Some possessed fear, shame, regret, or relief, and some, all of these at one time. I didn't know how I felt at the moment. As the process began, I thought I was doing the wrong thing, but as time passed, I understood why I needed to do this. This man was incapable of being the man I needed and wanted in my life, heading my family. The boys were already suffering from not feeling the love in their home. There was no need to draw another child into it. They gave us our medication, which knocked me out, no question. As I came in and out of consciousness, I saw girls coming and going since the room we were in was the holding room for those coming in and those going to have their procedure. Sitting there, I began to have regrets, but I stayed strong until they called my name. The transition staff assisted me as my legs were a bit wobbly from the medication. When we reached the procedure room, it looked as if I was going to have my yearly gyn exam. The funny thing about fear is when you're intoxicated by a drug, it will allow you to become aware of what is happening quickly. Although they told me to just relax, that thought was gone out of the window, and as they were ripping the human being from my body, I could feel what was happening to me. It was minutes that felt like hours, and when they were done, they asked me not to look to my left, which only made me look. What I saw was beyond disgusting, and at that moment, I felt ashamed of what I had done.

Slowly, the medication was wearing off, and as it was, tears began to fall that I did my best to hide. Most girls had a look of relief on their faces, and I was not about to judge them because of my regrets. What the people at the clinic don't do, which they should, is counsel you on how this could mentally be taxing on you afterward. They gave me a bag of birth control pills and prescriptions for pain meds and anti-biotics in a brown paper bag and told me what to do in an emergency but have a good day. When I got home Daniel began talking about how I killed his baby but walked out the door while telling me to call someone to get my meds. I was in so much pain physically, mentally, and emotionally that immediately I began praying and whaling for God to give my baby back. Now that I understand more about my emotions and manipulation, I understand this was exactly what he was trying to do. Daniel was not a father then, nor is he now, and here he was complaining about something he wasn't going to take time to raise to begin with. I thought it was me for a long time, but it was someone else pulling the strings. What I needed was for my husband to lay beside me and tell me it was going to be ok. Unfortunately, he used this time to make me feel worse even though he knew what I did benefited us both.

Whatever his reason for doing this to me, it worked, and I stopped my pills and started trying to get pregnant. Before I found out I was pregnant, our house was shot into, and once again, I saw Daniel was not a husband nor a protector. It started with me having fun and throwing firecrackers at Daniel and his friends. They were in the front yard playing cards, something they did consistently, and kept putting me off even though it was my birthday. What began as us having fun quickly turned into a "friend" of his starting to throw fireworks at the people across the street. Now, Jason was never good to Daniel, and I told him, but in true fashion, he didn't listen. This guy's spirit was one of evil and deceit, and Daniel found out about it too late. Jason knew those people and what would happen, yet he continued. After multiple screams from the neighbors and us asking them to stop, things changed when one of the fireworks hit a neighbor, Kim. Kim and her family were dealers and users also, so he knew he had made a bad mistake. Jason went over to apologize, but the damage was already done. She asked him several times to take it somewhere else, and he didn't, so she called family who came ready to kill anyone without understanding nor wanting to understand what happened. Following the exchange of a few words, everyone took a stance like out of the wild west and the women were told to get back right before gunshots rang out from both sides. No one was hit, but it wasn't because of a lack of effort. They were shooting back and forth before Daniel and the other guys ran behind the house, and we ran into the house. Not long after, you could hear shots ringing in my house as we all crammed between the fridge and the washing machine.

Thankfully someone heard and called the police, which was the only thing that stopped the shots. My dad was looking out the window and says he saw the guy standing at the front door shooting in the house and looking the other way. Therefore, I slept with the dresser up to the door and Daniel outside with a gun waiting for them to try and come back. A few days later, they came back, and all was forgiven, but I didn't trust that. I started spending most of my time indoors because of the anxiety I experienced when I walked out outside. Since I had no idea what they looked like, any suspicious car would bring me back to that night when my life was in the hands of someone other than me. Most importantly, I lost my job because I had gotten a ticket that I couldn't pay for, which led to my license being suspended. This was my second suspension, and with all the other refractions resulting from what was going on at home, I was terminated. It was the second time I had been terminated but needed this job this time. There was no going home as the drug and alcohol problem had ramped up. Also, I was a married woman, and Daniel was not going to live with my mom.

Now that Daniel was the breadwinner, he wasted no time exerting his superiority. So, when Camila came to me, looking for a place to stay and get away from my mom, I said yes. She was coming in tow, and unfortunately, I had to charge her for her stay. This was my way of having my own money and not have to ask Daniel. Her and my mom had been at each other's throat ever since I decided to leave. Camila saw what I was doing and was immolating it times 10. Also, she was very vocal about my mom's drinking and the individuals that were allowed to come in and do what they wanted. I hoped that this was temporary as the last thing we needed was another person in the house. I'd recently found out that I was pregnant again, so having them here was not ideal. To rush things along I spoke to my mom and found some sort of mediation for the time being. I understood my mom in saying that Camila was only 17 years old, but I knew that Camila was right but going about it the wrong way. She was concerned that they were getting high with her baby there displaying no respect. Now that this was no longer my problem, I focused on the bigger problem.

Once I found out Daniel was in fact selling crack, I was forced to erase that line in the sand. No longer was I in a position financially to live on my own with the boys. This meant him leaving us alone at night while I was still trying to overcome what happened. At first things were ok but then I learned Daniel was back with his old friend Adrian. I know that moving in silence is always better than a partnership with someone you haven't seen in years, not knowing what they'd been up to. However, Daniel saw Adrian as an opportunity to build this imaginary empire he was envisioning for this life. While that was his focus mine was getting out of here. Our home was crumbling inside and out, so I knew it was time for us to leave. Management changed and we were now dealing with a slum lord with a rumored drug problem himself, so nothing was getting fixed. The rental office was locked most of the time, and no one called you back. Eventually, the pool was shut down, our bathtub was severely stopped up, and the remnants of bullet holes still filled our walls. Outside, the traffic of drug dealing was becoming more evident as if it was every black male in our neighborhood new career opportunity. Thankfully, I found a job, but from the interview to first day was almost a month. As soon as I started working, I began looking for another place for us to live. It wasn't going to be easy now that I was making even less money and had only been working for two weeks. Leroy was nice enough to help; although it wasn't a mansion, we had a place to live.

The house was dated but had a yard where the kids could play safely. It was a two-bedroom one bath with a living room and dining room with walls and floors made of wood. Over time, the wood became depressing, but I was happy to be out of those apartments. While nothing was perfect, it was now manageable. Sorry to say it wouldn't last. My employment dropped from full-time to 2 ½ hours, which almost wasn't worth working. Starting a new job wouldn't make any sense until after I had the baby, so I stayed. I enjoyed working here, so I didn't put up too much fuss about leaving. There were only three of us, and most times, it was so slow that we just talked. It became more of a hangout spot than actual work.

Ben's habits had gotten worse, and he had become dependent on me bailing him out. Here I was struggling myself and trying to help someone who was able to help himself. Each time he promised to get help but as soon as he got paid; it was the same thing. This plus many other things put a strain on he and Missy's relationship. Not only was he messing up their life, but mine as well. Daniel saw me continuously helping and fussed about me stepping into something that didn't concern me.

Unk had also fallen hard times. He'd married his girlfriend some years back only now to be separated for reasons unknown. She took the one thing he loved, his Jaguar, and told him to kick rocks. He and my cousin Ray had gotten an apartment in Winston-Salem but were barely getting by. Ray was the only child of my aunt who passed before I got to know her. From what I've been told, she was the head of the family and well respected. My dad told me that their water and the lights were off. This was disappointing to hear because for as long as I could remember, my uncle was the one to have it all together. When that story was debunked, I saw him in a different light. Against logic I wanted to save him, so I took Daniel's car and asked my mom to ride just in case things went wrong. Somehow, I felt obligated to save him even when he was old and able to save himself.

When he first arrived, I was thrilled. This kept our disagreements at bay, and I had someone with me when Daniel was out all night. He went back and forth to Winston quite often as he was unwilling to let go of the life that no longer served him. Camila asked if I would throw her an 18th birthday party. At first, I was against it but changed my mind after speaking with Daniel. This was a wonderful time for her as she was receiving a settlement and wanted to open a hair salon. We talked about how we would partner to make this dream come true. Just like those before me, I supplied her with alcohol knowing it was not responsible. I also cooked and decorated with the help of Unk only for no one to show. She was disappointed as was I when Daniel suggested my greed was the only reason I threw her a party. Why he said this after he okayed me to do it was baffling to me. Yes, I did need her help in obtaining a car but, if need be, I would wait until tax time. This was his character though. One day he would be ok and the next minute he'd be upset. It was draining.

She and I had helped one another through some hard times and this time I needed her more than ever. Besides she didn't get the money until later so if she'd said no, the party was already done. When she received her money, she gave me $2500 to buy a 1991 burgundy Caprice Classic. She bought her a car as well and got her own place. She'd stop by but not as frequently now that she was doing well. I was happy for her and tried to guide her financially, but she was old enough to make her own decisions and that's what she did.

Daniel allowed me to take my maternity leave early. This was surprising but it was the one time I didn't put up a fight or ask questions. The only problem was having so much free time gave me time to think about my life. Stupidly, I thought this phase at home would allow us to spend time together, but he only had time for Adrian and the streets. He would fuss about me getting up when the boys were up because he had been out all night and wanted to sleep. Why would I want to lay there when he'd probably laid up with some chicken head the night before? It was horrible. I was supposed to be resting yet this was his major concern. He did surprise me and allow my cousins to have me a proper baby shower. It was the first time I had one but because of my unhappiness I couldn't appreciate it. The surprise was ruined when he wasn't available when they arrived, and I had to come unlock the door. They had done everything so this was the least he could do. I put on my mask of happiness and tried my best to enjoy the festivities. Even my mom stopped by which was unusual but welcomed.

Now that I was nine months, my appointments were weekly. I usually took myself, but I couldn't drive my car because I had a stripped lug nut that my brother was attempting to get loose. Daniel had given me his 22" rims and, in a rush, to put them on I had Ben to assemble them. He was in a rush too and didn't do a good job. I reluctantly asked Daniel because he always got up when I was leaving and not a minute before. He declined because he had to meet Adrian but insisted on paying Missy to take me. This was our typical exchange as we were almost roommates by this time. On the way back from a five-minute appointment, I received a phone call from him. He asked me how things went when he could have gone with me to find out. Adrian had flaked and not met him at their designated time. In the time it took me to get home, which was about 15 minutes, I heard some yelling with someone beating on the window, telling Daniel to get out. It was the police and they wanted him out of the car by any means necessary.

Frantically I kept asking Daniel who was that and what did they want. When he told me it was the police, I knew this was not good. Here, this man was talking to his wife, whom he neglected to be in this place, waiting for someone who could care less, and now he was on his way to jail. Karma definitely has a way of coming back on you.

Because of the arrest, Daniel decided to take it easy. He was home a little more which was surprising and welcoming. It was the first time I felt like a married couple. As we basked in the spring sun, I began having contractions. Once again, we were heading to the hospital to welcome our new addition. We left the boys at his mom's house so there were no distractions. When we arrived and they got me settled, they said we had a while. Immediately they gave me an epidural, so I was out of it from there. He decided that since there was nothing he could do, and we had time he would return. What was so important I will never understand but I said OK. Once things heated up, I called him because it wouldn't be long now. He brought the boys back as planned but because of the confusion, he missed the birth of our son, Dimarrius. He was angry and instead of coming in to check on me and the baby, he left. Again, I say, God will take something away from you that you take for granted.

Two weeks later Daniel was locked up again but this time with Adrian. Even though they bonded out that night, Daniel was now on their radar. In my heart I knew this was the beginning of the end. Things got interesting when Adrian hinted that Ben was the one to set them up. This was when I wished he had gone elsewhere to cop. I had known my brother to be a lot of things, but a snitch wasn't one of them.

While they plotted and planned on how they were going to beat this situation, I got to know his wife. She was in the same predicament with abuse and infidelity, but she was working toward a better life. She was the first woman I'd met who was willing to do what it took to free herself from this toxic behavior. While I wouldn't have considered us friends, I admired who she was as a woman. She went to school and had dreams of becoming a lawyer. We tried to lean on one another but was cut short when my life took a turn. Adrian's case was dismissed so Daniel was hopeful he would get the same deal. Tasha, Adrian's wife, picked me up and we rode out to get away from the world for the moment. She smoked and with everything going on, I thought I would join her today. It had been years since I'd indulged but I figured why not. We joked about going out and I was going to call Daniel to see if he was ok with that. Before I could call him, my cell rang. What I heard on the other end I had not bargained for. Daniel told me that the Feds were following him, and he was about to be arrested. WOW! Immediately, we went to where he was, and arrive to a parking lot of federal agents and local police tearing his car apart. This wasn't as simple as before; this was federal so there was no bond. It was back to planning visits.

As a wife, I knew I needed to stand by him, but as Brandy, I wanted to leave him down there and let him see how it felt. The months leading up to this incident my Friday nights consisted of getting wasted with my uncle and crying about this situation. Where was my husband? I don't know. The years of disrespect had wreaked havoc and I had done nothing to fix it. While I was contemplating how to handle everything, my phone started ringing. At first, they wouldn't say anything, but one day, they decided to be bold. I was visiting my mom when the phone rang. "When are you going to get my man out of county?" she said. OMG! Here we go for the umpteenth time. "If he's your man, then you go get him out," I replied. "You do know I'm sleeping with your husband," she responded. "And what would you like me to do about that?" I replied. "So, you don't care that I'm sleeping with your husband," she asked. "Why should I care?" I responded. "Well, I'm pregnant by him," she returned. "Ok, and what would you like me to do about that? My kids are good. That is between you and him," I explained to her. This was not the response she wanted from me, and became upset while stating, "You're stupid, you don't care about your husband sleeping with another woman and I am having his baby". "I absolutely do not because this has nothing to do with me," I responded. I asked her, "how did you get my number anyway?" and she replied, "he gave it to me for an emergency contact". Yeah ok.

This went on and on the entire time Daniel was in county. I told him, but he declared that he knew nothing. This was not my first rodeo, so I knew it was a lie, but I continued to play my part. After some time, the judge was nice enough to let him out on supervised release. This meant an ankle monitor with a curfew and he was to gain employment. I won't say that I was upset with their temporary sentencing because this meant he was forced to sit down. Not long after his release, the unknown call came in again, so I reached him the phone in hopes of finally stopping the calls. He distorted his voice, and I knew then he knew exactly who it was. I rolled my eyes and went back to being a mom to my children. It was like Tina and Ike in that I felt bad leaving him at his worst, but what about my worst. He gave no real remorse for the pain he had me suffer through. He must've reached out to her because the calls stopped.

From what I understood, the lawyer was not talking about freedom. He stated the chances of him going free were slim unless he came up with a lot of money. We had to wait on the discovery before he could discuss anything more, so Daniel decided it was time we prepared for him to go to prison. I wanted to go to hair school, but because I had taken some money from him, which was no doubt for the house, he told me he wouldn't help me. He decided I should go to Medical Assisting school, which I did. What's funny was this cost the same as Cosmetology school but I said nothing. I also worked part-time at Walmart. 2004 proved to be the most stressful time for me, and it started to take out my hair and mess with my blood pressure. I don't know how I made it through school because I barely had enough time to study. I still had motherly and wife duties at home, and it was driving me mad. To add to my stress, one day, I came home and noticed my wedding pictures were not on the mantle. That was strange but even more so when I found them under the chair in the living room. I questioned the children about someone being in the home, and fearfully, D told me. TF!!! Why didn't he leave already?! I didn't have to, as this was my place in my name, and it was clear we were not meant to be together. Why were both of us being tolerant of one another? It wasn't until he thought I set him up for someone to rob us because I got off work early and surprised him that I understood.

My mom had to move to the extended stay up from our house because her house caught on fire. Not sure who was to blame but it was the result of someone leaving a burning crack pipe in a chair in the room. Thank God no one was hurt but my mom lost everything. Now that they were up the street it only made things worse. She was a help with the boys but as soon as the theft happened, Daniel stopped wanting her there for fear she was the culprit. I didn't believe this but again he helped with the house and was my husband, so I chose a side. What I learned was I was still living in fear, and he was able to walk all over me. Once again, he put his hands on me. Slapping me so hard he burst an abscess that was on my gums, and as I fell to the ground crying, he decided to kick me.

I graduated by the grace of God. The ten months it took me to finish this course was filled with continued stress, and I just wanted it to be over. I was praying for something I didn't want. I was doing what everyone expected of me and being the wife, he didn't deserve. Both sides of the family showed up for my graduation. The relationship with his family had softened but I was still on guard. Daniel threw the best graduation party and most of my cousins showed up. I was thrilled and made sure it was a night to remember. During my externship I had taken a job opportunity so that Monday it was off to the real world.

After a few weeks of the boys taking care of Dimarrius, my mom moved to our neighborhood, and I asked if she could babysit. This helped immensely because I didn't have to rush home worried, they had gotten into something. Daniel was able to get a job at a Warehouse so I hoped we could get the money. Besides my personal feelings my boys deserved their father, and I wanted this marriage to get better. Maybe this was the lesson he and I needed to get things right. We sat down and talked over how to get this money, but he later decided he wasn't going to do that. Instead, he was going to put our life in the hands of the government and take whatever they produced for us. This was another selfish move but typical of someone out to beat a system they don't know the rules for. This was not a good idea with the Mandatory Minimum Guidelines being used for drug offenders.

Before school started back, Unk moved in with us full-time. He job was to get D and Davion off to school and babysit Dimarrius. This was helpful especially since he kept the house clean and cooked when I asked. My only responsibility was to get the boys clothes ready at night and he took it from there. Also, most mornings I was forced to deal with Daniel's attitude. It occurred so often that I started ignoring him and let him speak when he was ready. His reasoning was dealing with the fact that he was going to prison, and I couldn't relate. He wanted me to prepare for the worst, but I was trying to be optimistic. Coming to the reality that your husband was about to go to prison was not something I wanted to deal with. The only good thing out of this was the amount of attention he showed the boys. We had our time, so even if this time with the boys was temporary, they could say they knew what it was like to spend time with their father.

In true Daniel fashion, nothing is ever what it seems. While I was feeling bad that I couldn't connect with how he must be feeling, he was entertaining another woman. All of this was revealed when she called on his phone New Years Eve. 2006 was starting off wrong and I'd had about enough. I reminded him that he was facing a lot of time and if he wanted me to stand by him, he was to make a choice. What a joke!

{ 11 }

Time's Up

Why did I need to remind him of what he had to lose? If he didn't know he didn't deserve it anyway. We were nearing the end of this two-year court battle when they decided to give him time to give them something or get his affairs in order. I think this was the worst thing they could have done for our family, but they were only concerned with him doing something for them. Another cousin of his started visiting more and sometimes the night. I couldn't say much as my uncle and cousin now lived with us. Not to say I chose my cousin over his because I was ready for him to leave as well. My issue was the cousin sleeping on the first set of furniture that resembled a home instead of the $200 leather we purchased every tax year because it was so cheap. My voice was muffled again because he was "free" and felt back in control. He defended what was happening, even going so far as to put me in my place in front of his cousin. I let him win and focused on the fact that they both would be gone soon. They stayed out all hours of the night doing who knows what and I allowed it until it came to my house. While they were out one night, I was awakened by the terrifying screams of my uncle telling me someone was shooting into our home. I thought I dreamt the pinging noises and the sound the bullets made as they sped past. The holy spirit was with us because each bullet hole was an inch above my and my children's heads. So much so that if we had awakened at the time of the shooting, we would have been shot. I was petrified and furious at the same time. I was walking in a circle, trying to understand what was happening. Wait...where was my husband? I called and called, but no answer. I reached out to his brother where the same thing happened, and Kisha informed me as to why.

Now I was even more furious because he was supposed to be thinking of us and getting things together, yet he was out starting a war. A war that had nothing to do with defending your wife and kids but your cousin. If it were not evident before it was written plain now that the only person Daniel cared about was Daniel. Everyone else was collateral damage on his plight to prove to himself who he was because no was else was questioning this. Not long after I hung up the phone with them, he arrived disheveled, and even though I told him what happened, he showed no desperation to find out who would do this. I played dumb just to see what his reaction would be. He showed no remorse for his part in almost taking the lives of five people.

This was the second time I feared for my life and this time my children's lives, so I decided I was done living here. Especially since I knew his allegiance was not with his wife and children. He thought he could silence me by taking us to a hotel for a few nights, but I wasn't satisfied. Thankfully a postcard came promoting home ownership and I called immediately. He was reluctant, but because of him, I no longer felt safe when he went to prison. While I understood that the rent here was much more manageable than a house payment, I was willing to take my chances.

The process was problematic since I didn't have great credit. They did what they could so that we both were on the loan, but I didn't care if he signed alone, he owed us this. We'd tried homeownership before but didn't finish the process. They were building a neighborhood not too far from our house in Oakdale. I enjoyed looking at different homes seeing how I would decorate when I found out I was pregnant again. After all we had gone through there was no way I was going to have that baby. It was back to the abortion clinic for me and this time I felt relieved. So much so I paid and drove myself there and back.

August arrived and it was closing time. I received a call that we had to bring closing cost. No one explained this to me prior otherwise I could have put away for it. I knew he wouldn't be happy about this, so I waited until we got there and let them tell him. I knew this was not how we needed to communicate but this is where we were. He told them he had it but had to go home and get it. While this was supposed to be the happiest day of our lives, I helped make it just a day. When we got home, he told me this was his money he was saving to take with him to prison. Wait. So not only were you going to prison for some hair brained scheme for you, but you were also saving money for you. I walked away from the conversation as if he hadn't said a word. He always kept money from me, so this wasn't new it was the reasoning that made me roll my eyes. My focus was more that my children safe and were able to have a new home which was something neither one of us had experienced.

Moving was an experience since I decided I didn't want anyone to know where we lived. I rented an SUV for the excess things that didn't need to go on the moving truck. My cousin had proved himself to want nothing more, so I was not willing to take that baggage with me. Daniel let his cousin stay at the old place to clean it up. I'm not certain that happened but I took his word for it. It was as if time was reset, and we were on the right path for becoming a healthy family. My car needed a transmission, so I was forced to get a new car just before we moved. We were still riding to work together and spent the weekends doing things around the house. It was finally a calm environment until it wasn't.

BJ had asked to stay the weekend which was new for us. It was also a teacher workday so it would be a long weekend. His mom and I kept in touch since my brother was mostly absent. Another issue Daniel had but kept silent for the most part. Partially because he thought BJ was my child that my family was keeping a secret. Nevertheless, he was getting older and exerting disrupting behavior and I thought this would be the perfect opportunity for me to talk some sense into him.

Everything was fine until it was bedtime and Daniel decided to remind me to make sure he got in the bed. This was comical but I didn't want to argue. Since we went to bed around nine, I told BJ to make sure he cut off the TV and was in the bed by 10. We both went to bed with me thinking he would comply. The next day we awakened to my nephew doing exactly what I'd told him not to. Instantly Daniel shifted the blame to me and while his feelings were valid why not just tell him instead of telling me while I was taking a shower. When I finished getting dressed, I woke him and told him to go get in the bed. Daniel stormed out the door, so I knew this was going to be another long ride. Silently we got in the car, but it didn't last. As soon as we turned the first corner leading out of the neighborhood he started. He cursed me hard at 7am on the way to work and ended with, "Bitch take me to work before I slap the shit out of you". It was a hard pill to swallow, but I did. Of course, he called after I got to work to apologize. We had received his court date that was two weeks from that day, so I just counted down.

That same week I found out I was pregnant but miscarried a week before his court day. The morning of his court day, I replayed all that happened since we moved here and figured it was for a reason. I also thought about how silly he was going to feel if they locked him up which was almost certain. This time we took the boys, and his mom met us there. After all I had endured, I wanted nothing more than for them to give us more time. I wasn't ready to be a single parent or my kids to be fatherless. For better or worse, he was my husband but the plan for my life was not to be his wife. God had shown me time and time again, but I was in the damn way. He decided the only way for him to save me was to remove the distraction. Before we moved, I had spoken with my dad about living with him if this time came to which his wife told him she would pay my rent if I stayed. Although she helped him in no way, he agreed to her suggestion knowing she was not about to live up to her word. That wasn't my path either, so I let go of the resentment not long after.

In The Damn Way

The judge sentenced him to 360 months, and I couldn't believe my ears. Not only that but he was to be remanded. "This is BS" I shouted before we left the courtroom. I left the courtroom feeling defeated and cried all the way home. When I arrived, it was time to boss up. He left me with nothing, I had nothing, so there was no reason to continue moping. I thought that our families would rally around us, but that was not the case. His job provided more support than anyone. They gave me his last paycheck and his bonus plus gifts for the children during Christmas. They vowed to make sure the kids had Christmas while their dad was away and a job for him when he got out.

In the meantime, there was a mortgage and bills that had to be paid. It was time I budgeted how I spent my money as much as possible. Since I was never good with budgets it didn't help that I was now the sole provider. He was in county for a while so spending money for visits was minimum for now. He had taken some money with him, so I didn't need to worry about commissary needs. Unk was back in Winston for the time being, so I had to take the boys to my mom's house for school. I had to pay her too which was overextending my funds, but I had to do what was necessary. I put my game face on and decided not to let anyone see me sweat.

I decided to put my Caprice in the shop to rid myself of my car payment. Daniels sister needed a car, so I trusted her to take over the payments. When the car was ready, I borrowed the money from my mom until I got my tax money. Also, I thought it was better if I spent most of my time over his mom's house. This way no one could accuse me of anything and if I missed a call, he could catch me here. Even though he was the one doing all of the cheating, I was the one making sure he was happy and suspected nothing. Outside of me needing my mom for something I spent as little time with her as possible. While I could only hope she was respectful when my kids were there, I knew for a fact she wasn't after I picked them up. Most times I would walk in see she was high and leave rather than stay and get upset. Camila was now having similar issues with staying afloat now that her funds were dwindling. She no longer wanted to stay with my mom either and did her best to stay gone when she left.

Whenever my uncle resurfaced, I reminded him that his help was now needed more than ever. I could no longer support him, and he needed to get a job. In the meantime, they had transferred Daniel, and I was visiting every other weekend. We stayed the weekend because of the time it took to get there and the amount of time for the visit. This caused even more financial strain, but I was so focused on pleasing Daniel that I didn't think of the irreparable damages I was making for myself. On top of that I sent him money after he'd blown through what he'd saved. I was hopeful he would get out on appeal, and I didn't want any crap when he got out about this or that. I was trying my best to show him I was committed, although I didn't know why because he never did. He had told me he didn't want me to attend church as the men of the church would try to hit on me. I obliged even though he didn't deserve what I was giving.

In the meantime, and between times, my uncle was working on my last nerve. For some reason, he wasn't thrilled to help me and felt like he was doing me a favor. How so when I'm giving you a place to live? He worked about a mile from the house and thought I should let him drive my car to work at night. Ummm no! No one helped me fix it, and now because you're paying me $400, you want to drive my car to do what you should have done long ago. It was my fault that I made his life so comfortable, but now it was time to be comfortable about being uncomfortable. He wasn't the only one. My brother was still coming to me asking me for this or that, as if I was not a newly single parent and homeowner with three kids to think about. My dad was charging me to cut my grass because he had a lawn service, and I was receiving no help from him. The amount I could endure was unbelievable, but I knew it would come to a head sooner or later. It wasn't long before my uncle lost his job, and it was back on me to pick up the slack. After a few months of not being able to keep up, I had to succumb to my loss and watch my home go into foreclosure. I remembered the good times as I packed my things from this three-bedroom home to move into the two-bedroom apartment. I didn't know if this was my last home, but I couldn't think about that too much. I had to move forward.

We hadn't lived in an apartment like this in five years. It was a two-bedroom, two-bath flat, and I didn't have to give up any amenities. It was a lot smaller, but it freed up some funds, and now that I was making more money, it was manageable. My uncle was still not working, so I was grateful for the change. Over Thanksgiving break, we went to Winston Salem to spend time with my dad at my stepsister's house. Unbeknownst to me, my uncle decided to stay after he told me he would come back with my dad, who was staying an extra day. The lie detector test determined that it was a lie (in my Maury voice), and he didn't come back or call to say anything. It was understandable. The men in my life were cowards, so it made sense. I kept moving, which was the only thing I knew to do. I felt like if he wanted to stay, that was on him, but I wasn't going to rescue him this time. Christmas came, and the boys had a wonderful time, as usual. Seeing them happy was the only thing that kept me sane through the constant trials and tribulations.

The new year came in, and I hoped it would be better than the last two. Who was I to think that my troubles ended with the turn of a new year? As the songwriter wrote, "it ain't over until God says it's over". Unk was still a no show which was fine because watching him lay there while I went to work was getting to me. At this point I was ready to put him out, but I still wanted to give him the benefit of the doubt to show up for us. I put my guard down for a half second, and it was a mistake. As luck would have it, I needed some new brakes on the car, and I had let it go on long enough.

It was January 2008 when my life started lifeing in a way that I couldn't control. I had only been in this apartment two months and was proud of myself for paying the bills on time. I called Ben to fix the brakes knowing he was inexpensive, and I could trust him to get it right. He was okay with completing the work while I was at work, but I had another favor to ask. It was the fifth, and I needed to pay my rent, so I asked if he could get a money order and drop it off. He obliged so I got my mom to drop me off and he would pick my car up from her house. She asked me was I sure about this for which I replied, "Yes". He had done nothing to make me believe anything otherwise. After a complete thought I asked her if she would accompany him to make sure it was done, and she said "Yes". At lunch time I decided to call to make sure my rent was paid. It started out with him saying my mom said she was going to do it and her saying he left her. The last thing I needed was the run around about my money for the rent. I could have done without the brakes. Since he said he would go back and get the money I let it be and went back to work. There was an uneasiness that fell upon me that I hadn't felt since Daniel went to prison. The last conversation we had was him assuring me that my rent was paid, and he was on the way to get the brakes.

Finally, it was five o'clock and all of uneasiness would be put to rest when he picked me up with my rent receipt and no more squealing brakes. I walked outside to no Ben and now he wasn't answering the phone. No, no, no, this was not happening to me! I called my mom in hopes that he was there, but she hadn't seen him since that morning. I reluctantly asked her a question I knew the answer to and that was did she go with him to pay the rent. "No" she responded and if I wasn't afraid that I would get hurt I probably would have fainted right there. This was not happening, but it was and there was nothing I could do about it.

He and Missy had broken up not long after I gave birth to Dimarrius. When he came to buy from Daniel, he was with another woman I didn't know. He introduced her as his friend, and I left it at that. She never said much until it was apparent that they were a couple. Her name was Ashley, and she was not the normal woman my brother dated. She had gone to college, owned her home, and worked for corporate America. At first glance she was someone I admired and aspired to become until I found out she was no better than the rest. While she wanted the best for my brother, she enabled him. He would take her car and stay gone for the weekend while she stayed at my mom's. Quickly I deduced that she was his cash cow rather it was true or not.

Because they were always together, I figured if anyone knew where he was it was her. She got off around the same time, so I called her to interrogate what she knew and ask for a ride home. All the times he left her at my mom's or at work and I picked her up, I was always angry and defending her. Now that it was me, she didn't possess the same energy and I immediately thought she knew where he was even when she precluded that she didn't. She dropped me at my mom's and while I wanted to break down and cry, I yelled and cursed instead. Somehow, she was able to track him down and I demanded that she take me to him at once. What would you know he was in Lakeview which was where my life turned for the worse to begin with. This was very ironic that this was place he chose to hide out. She went in to get him and as she was talking to him, I jumped out questioning what was happening and why he was hiding from me. He was way to calm which probably meant he was already high, and I asked him the one question I regretted. "Did you pay my rent?" He said "Yes", and I wanted to believe him, but something in my gut told me it was a loss. I told him if he was lying, I was coming back, and it was not going to be pretty. He assured me that he would never steal from me and until the next day, I had no way of knowing if that were true. I got my keys and went back to my moms to pick up the boys and go home. Ashley wanted to continue talking about it, but I just wanted to go home and wish this day never happened.

The next morning at 9:00 am on the dot, I called the rental office only to hear what I feared. There was no rental payment. I immediately called Ben, but his girlfriend said he was gone. Gone?? My first thought was, why did you let him leave? What was I going to do? There was no one I could borrow the money from. Even if I could, there was not enough left over to pay them back, so that was out of the question. I'd filed my tax return with my last paystub so there was no other money coming in. Ok this meant I was going to have to sacrifice to get back on track.

Ben came back a few days later with none of my money and no apology for his actions. He was so crass he wouldn't even speak to me on the phone. It was as if I had done something to make him take this money from me. All this from the same person I'd helped consistently when he binged, got sick, or he and Ashley didn't have a car and I let them use mine. OK! This was when I knew I had no one in my corner. NO ONE tried to help, and he was never outcasted for his actions. Everyone moved on so I thought I may as well as I couldn't live on an island just yet. Exactly a month after Ben took my rent money, I was getting ready for work and sent D outside to crank up the car. "Ma, the car is not out there," he said. Being that it was an apartment complex and I usually parked in different places, I responded "It's across the parking lot facing the house." "It's not there," he stated. Irritated that I didn't have time for this, I snatched my keys and decided to do it on my own. To my surprise, he was correct. My car was gone! You have got to be kidding me. First my money and now my car. I called my brother to help me, but he never showed up. However, my dad did show up this time. This only added to the fuel, and my first thought was that Ben had something to do with that as well. Whoever took it knew I left one door unlocked because the driver door wouldn't unlock from the outside. Only people who had driven my car knew this. On top of that, there was no glass from a busted window on the ground. Now that doesn't prove my case, but his not showing up ran my conspiracy. We dropped the kids off for the bus, and I called the doctor I worked for. I told her I wasn't going to be there today. I had to search for my car. After a few hours, she called me back and asked me how much I needed to find a car. I appreciated her wanting to help me but didn't want to ask for too much. My pride was too strong from not having real help, and this was unfamiliar territory. I didn't need another car payment. I was barely making it as is, but in a rush, I had to do what was necessary. I tried my best to find something I could pay for but was unsuccessful. Instead of taking a moment to understand what I needed and letting everyone wait for me to figure that out, I put them first and asked my dad to take me to Statesville to get a car. Because of my credit, I had a device on my car that would shut my car down if I didn't make my car payment. It was an embarrassment to myself, but I held my head high and continued to do what I needed to do.

My stress level was steadily rising, and it was only a matter of time before it blew up in my face. I had to take some of my money for my rent to add to what I was blessed with to make the down payment for the car. This poked a hole in my plan to sacrifice and make two rental payments to catch up from the last screw up. I didn't understand what God was doing, but I was getting very upset with what I was experiencing. What upset me more was that no one was on my side. I had allowed my family to condition me to always be there for them no matter what. Instead of my feelings being validated about Ben, the conversation turned out to make it all my fault. I take the blame for trusting someone, but I didn't make him take my money. Because I had been there for him through all his bad, I was delusional enough to think I was omitted from his shenanigans. All I got was to get over it. We're family. I did it. I needed my family, especially with the children. My only option was to suppress my emotions with everything else and keep moving.

Although my family was no help in truly being a support system, they were specialists in gossiping behind my back. Word got back that my stepsister knew my husband had a child. She confirmed what she said, only for his sister to ask me, "Who told you?". Wait, so ya'll know too, and no one said anything to me. "Well, I was told not to say anything, but the child was born around the time Davion was born," she continued. Now, the problem with these two answers was that they meant more than one child. The girl who was making claims about the baby wasn't old enough to fit the timeline of the child his sister was speaking about. This husband of mine was continuing to be a pain on my side, and he was in prison. I knew he would say no if I asked because he was prone to deny even when I caught him red-handed.

The level of betrayal my life was revealing was taking a toll on me physically. On top of that I was dealing husband who left me nothing, wanting everything, who told me he was not going to help parent because it was not helpful. It was like I was stuck in the twilight zone but there was no ending. So much so that I started having chest pain that was followed by numbness in my face and arm. I was tipping over and the only suggestion my doctor had was high blood pressure or anxiety medicine. I couldn't continue stretching my heart to this limit without causing irreversible effects. The truth was I needed to let go of everyone and focus on myself, but I wasn't sure I could do that just yet. After months of continuous drama and anger, I decided enough was enough and told my brother I was coming to stay with them. I thought I would get better if I could just escape everything. I figured it was the least he could do since he was the one who caused this new onset of stress. Besides, he wasn't trying to pay me back, and I felt like I would make him apologize and admit to his wrongdoing. He didn't, and it didn't help me to be there hoping he would.

The conversation surrounding whether my husband had another child wouldn't die as the woman who was talking continued to keep this topic relevant. Eventually I asked him about it but just as I suspected he denied it. Subsequently, I found some work friends that I could be myself with and enjoyed every moment of it. Although one of the women was an ex of Daniel's, I didn't let it bother me. As a matter of fact, I told her I would hook them back up. This was how bad I was over this whole situation. It wasn't just enough to be married; I was ready to be happy. The only problem with that is I didn't know what that felt like, as it had been so long since I truly felt that way. Since nothing was truly getting better, I took my doctor's advice and started taking anxiety medicine. Maybe this would help me get the happiness I was longing for. I also used my employee assistance program to talk to a neutral person. They had me take a survey to assess my needs only to discover I was severely depressed. No wonder nothing I did helped me feel better. This meant depression medication which I wasn't flattered about but wanted badly to feel better.

For my birthday I decided I wanted to go out to a club. Finally, I was feeling better and wanted to let my hair all the way down. It was visiting day for Daniel, and I went alone. Two years of me making sure I was the perfect wife was about to come to an end. I left that visit different than I came. As I looked in the rearview, I knew this life was slowly becoming a part of my past. This man deserved someone, but it wasn't me any longer. He could probably feel it coming too but I never asked. The problem was I wasn't quite sure I was ready so for now it was only a thought. That night Ben drove as I broke the chains of being someone's stepping stool. I broke every rule imaginable even sleeping with a co-worker.

In the beginning, things were scary because they were new, and I was still afraid Daniel would find out. Please don't misunderstand. I'm neither proud nor ashamed of what I did as a married woman. The problem was I forgot I was still responsible for three children. Not that I neglected them totally, but I was absent where I should've been present. Every weekend, I was drinking or going out and spending until I was almost broke. I needed a new outfit, hair done, and top shelf liquor all night. I was doing what was done to me without thinking it was wrong. For a while, I was only thinking of what I needed and not focusing on why I was getting up every day. It's tough being in a position where you are hurt and mad and no one has taught you to deal with your emotions. You speak up and say you're hurting, and everyone blames you for being too extra or dramatic and to just calm down. My actions were screaming for someone to help me, but no one was listening.

Soon I began to think if I could hurt someone and treat them the way I was treated then it would make me feel better. So, I met Darrien who I knew had nothing, so he should have been lucky he had someone like me. He was fresh out of prison so I was arrogant enough to make him believe I would blow up my life for him when I had no intentions. We met at the club/bar that had now become a favorite of mine. He was a crush that me and my coworker/friend Sasha had but I stole for no reason other than selfishness. I was having sex with him and acting like he wasn't good enough for that on the weeks I was going to see Daniel. Being able to deal with him on my terms made me feel like I had some power. That's not to say he wasn't benefiting from sleeping with other women, but the way I was acting was not my character at all.

Trying to hide who I had become was starting to show. Financially I was worse off than ever which resulted in pawning my ring and buying it back right before I went for my visit. I also sold my furniture to Megan for $200. What I didn't know is this is what it meant to be addicted to something. Addicts use every play in their arsenal to feed their addiction and I was no different. While I couldn't see what I was doing my dad quickly recognized that I had a problem and reeled me in. He literally saved my life and my relationship with my children. I could deal with the world judging me but not them. He told me about a three-bedroom house that was perfect for us. The park was right behind our house, but there was also a big enough backyard for them to play in. I started seeing a psychologist that was tweaking my medication to help me see clearly. I hated the way it made me feel. It's like I could feel my brain being overtaken by this drug, but if it helped, I was going to take it. There was just one problem. Identifying you have a problem and getting help is only half of the solution. The other half was being honest about what was the root of it all and I was not ready for that conversation. I stopped seeing the psychologist but continued taking the medication.

The six months I spent at my brothers was over and, in a month, I was back in my own place. Life was easing back to some type of normalcy, and I was ready to receive it. All we had was our beds since I sold the living room furniture but that was fine. Just like everything in my life this wouldn't last long. Kisha sold me her Tahoe that was hit by the shooting years earlier and she had no interest in fixing. The car payment was interfering with my financial security, so I was thrilled about getting rid of it. Darrien was slipping away so I decided to keep him by suggesting we try to be in a relationship. This was not going to work but I pretended it would. It wasn't long before my mom needed a place to stay because they had bedbugs. Leroy stayed at their apartment as he was not getting bit and wanted to keep their place. To accommodate I let her take D's room and put the boys back together in one room. Not long after Leroy joined, and I gave them my room that had a bathroom and took the extra room. I told them not to bring any of their things and gave them my bed too. A friend of mine worked for BestWay furniture rental, so anytime I needed something else to accommodate these people he helped me get it.

Unk made it back and he too needed a place to stay. I put him in the room with the boys. This was not what I expected when I moved back on my own. Darrien's daughter had come down for the summer and since he was here almost daily, so was she. I told Daniel that I loved Darrien and no longer wanted to be with him. This was who I had become now that I no longer cared what anyone thought of me. While I was enjoying this time with Darrien my mom decided she was the woman of my house. No one paid me to live here yet when the cable was cut off, she decided to raise her voice at me. To keep the peace Darrien and I left for the night. It was time everyone found their own place because this was not going to work. Not only that, but they also slowly turned my house to the hangout spot. As if I wanted to come home to blasting music and everyone drunk already.

Spring approached and my dad offered Unk a job with him. He'd been laid off from his job and instead of getting a new one, he started his own landscape business. It had been a year, and it was doing well so he thought he would give Unk some work. While out, Unk stepped on a nail which developed into severe chest pain that next morning. I called 911 and met him at the hospital. I don't know the connection of the two, but that incident led to us finding out he had Stage IV lung cancer. My mouth dropped when I saw the half-dollar sized spots on his lungs. They gave him 18 months to live.

Overextending myself and my finances led to me looking for another place to live. The owners tried to get me to stay but I was too far gone to catch up. Darrien had gotten himself together and met someone during the time we were together and now was leaving to be with her. I was hurt but I deserved it all. I told Daniel who convinced me that he knew it wouldn't last because it wasn't real. He felt like the depression medication was taking a toll on me causing me to make rash decisions. I agreed, apologized, and said we could work it out. The reality was even though Darrien and I didn't work out that didn't mean I wanted Daniel.

One thing I knew I wasn't taking all these people with me. Both Unk and my mom were secretly trying to convince me why I should take them with me. Unk was not getting any income yet, so I took my mom. I also called Daniel's brother and told him to come get his things. I was done lugging his things along with me when I didn't know if I wanted to be with him anymore. I found a 3 bedroom 2-bathroom duplex in East Charlotte by Mint Hill. A week after moving, Leroy's unemployment was cut off and now they could no longer pay me either. This was a mess. Once again, my mom thought this was her house and confronted the landlord. This was a no no since she wasn't on the lease and couldn't help paying for anything. It didn't matter because in one month I moved from here too. I couldn't afford this by myself, and I no longer wanted my mom to live with me. The landlord understood and after meeting my mom felt sympathy for me and allowed me to move out without affecting my rental history.

{ 12 }

Reset

Reluctantly I asked Camila if we could live with her while I looked for a new place. The first week I found a place, but it would take two weeks before we could move in. She had never asked me for money but as soon as she saw me spend $50 for some shoes, she came asking. I gave it to her but couldn't wait until it was time to go. My uncle moved in with her after I moved but now wanted to move with me. He was receiving social security, so I figured this was ok. When it was time to go, I was thrilled. They had rehabbed the apartments on Key St., and I was one of the first one's moving in. Slowly it began to fill up with cousins which made coming home from work fun. Most days we sat on the porch listening to music and having a few beers before retiring for the night.

I met a new guy Ricki, who was Sasha's brother. He was younger than me and didn't live in Charlotte, so this was perfect. Also, he was in a relationship so I knew he couldn't hurt me. A few months after me, Camila moved to the neighborhood and my mom was with her. This was not what I needed but what choice did I have. Unk continued smoking even though he was going through Chemo, and it was upsetting me. I had to understand this was his life so if that's what he chose who was I to say anything. Once again it was a lot to handle at one time, but I managed to use Ricki as a way out of reality.

November 2009 was the biggest party I'd ever thrown. It was Unk's birthday and he decided on a huge party. I invited Ricki who invited some of his friends too. I was so busy flirting with him and being cute that I forgot it wasn't my day. Unk reminded me that it was his night as we laughed it off and posed for a picture to capture the moment. The boys were over Daniel's moms house, so I asked Ricki if he wanted to stay the night. No matter what, I vowed to not let my life mix with the life I had with my children. I had done this before, and it didn't work so I was not going through that again. Besides, they had a dad even if he had relinquished his position until his release.

The next day Unk started to experience pains that got worse as the days passed. It was hard seeing him in pain when there was nothing I could do to help. We made it through the holidays before he was in and out of the hospital. The doctors said there was nothing they could do without putting him in a coma. The 18 months had been shortened as the cancer was spreading. We decided to get tattoos after we went to file my much-needed divorce, but he was in too much pain to get out of the car. February 26, 2010, while I was getting ready to receive him at the hospice center, Unk passed. It was the most heartbreaking moment I had experienced since the day I saw my dad turn into a crackhead. He showed up for me when my parents didn't and now, he was gone. Now what?

Once Daniel's family found out I divorced him they flipped on me. They all thought I divorced him because I wanted to be free. This was the furthest from the truth. What they didn't know and neglected to find out before they passed judgement was the girl who made trouble about being pregnant by him had taken my place on social media and he had deleted me. He kept my sister, added this woman/girl, and deleted his wife and that was the last time I allowed him to play me in my face. Sure, I was having fun, but I was also making sure he was ok. On top of I should've made this decision long before then. His job followed suit and stopped helping me with Christmas for the boys. This was hilarious but I kept living.

I had become dependent on Unk's half of the bills and spent frivolously. When he died, he didn't leave me anything and his funeral arrangements was left for me to handle. Somehow my dad didn't feel he needed to help and took the money left in Unk's wallet that could have been used to help. My only option was cremation, but I had to track down two of his three children to do so. I hadn't seen them since I was four but luckily, we found them. The other issue was one was in Rock Hill and the other Columbia, SC. After sending him off the best way I could it was back to living and I wasn't ready for that.

Ricki had proposed to his girlfriend, so he and I saw a little less of one another. It wasn't long before there was someone taking his place. Being alone was not on my mind anymore. The neighborhood was no longer the same and because I wasn't paying bills like I should have we moved. This time I found a place before moving out but had to stay the night at Camila's before we moved in. The place was smaller than where I was even though it was 3-bedroom 2 ½ bath. It was off Avalon which wasn't any better than where we were. What I didn't know was that Camila wasn't paying her rent and before we could get in good, needed to move in. By this time, she had three kids, and I was not for this. Once again, I was taking away from my children to give to someone else. That's not to say I didn't need her at times, but I was always in transition. She had no other options, so she needed time.

I found out that the hot water was ran by gas. I had a previous bill that had to be paid before I could get the gas on. I was barely getting by, so I didn't have any extra money. During the summer it was ok but once it started to get cool, I had to make a choice. We had to heat water on the stove, and it was manageable until D dropped the water on himself. I'm sure he had some third degree burns that I treated at home so the hospital wouldn't call social service on me. That's when someone at work told me about borrowing from my 401(k). I borrowed what I could in hardship and called to pay the bill. Right before they were going to cut the gas on the motor went out on my car at the same time the rent was due. I couldn't believe that this was happening right when I thought I had it all figured out.

Camila had moved so there was no one to keep an eye on the boys if I caught the bus. In the neighborhood we lived in, I was NOT going to let my kids catch the bus by themselves, and besides, no one would be there to put Dimarrius on the bus. I opted to move in with my mom until I got another car and found another place to move. She and I still had a strained relationship, so I wasn't thrilled about moving with her. She had gone through some tragic things the last few years and had given up crack but still drank heavily.

Finding a car and a place was not going to be easy but I was determined. I caught the bus to work, and a coworker dropped me off. My mom and I were already bumping heads and it was getting worse. So much so that I came home and drank until I was drunk so I could go to sleep. She did her best to make sure we didn't feel welcome. After all I did when she was out, and this was how she repaid me. This was befitting with how she treated me growing up, so I dealt with it. I signed up for school to get some financial aid, so I had the money to get what I needed. From paying my mom, drinking, and paying for rides everyday my money was not adding up to be anything. Finally, I found a car and within a month a place to stay. It couldn't have come at a better time since Leroy was beginning to take his frustrations out on my boys and that's a no no.

By the time we moved, we had nothing and that was ok. It was February 2011, and I was just thrilled to have a place far away from my family. Tion, my friend at BestWay, held my bed so I didn't have to pay for storage. As soon as I got off, I told the boys let's go. I thanked my mom even though she made it uncomfortable and off we went. When we got home, I sat the boys down and explained that I was deeply sorry for everything I had taken them through. They were just so happy that they had a place to call home again. It was a two-bedroom townhome with a private patio for which I was thankful. I needed some time to seclude myself from everyone and finally figure out my plan. We stopped, got us some food, sat on the floor, and enjoyed one another. Before we made the floor our bed that night, I looked them in the eyes and made them a promise. I told them this was our home, and I would do everything to ensure this is where we stayed. If we left, it was going to be in a home that I purchased for us. I could see the happiness in their eyes as they gave me a hug, we said our love you, prayed, and went to bed. There was a problem I was refusing to face: how was I going to accomplish something I had never seen done? I didn't know how to love, was mad as hell at the world, and had no trust in anyone. BUT GOD!!

Interlude

I felt blood gushing from a wound i couldn't find yet was seemingly omnipresent; i found myself in a prison of glass, the same blood occupying every corner of the room, inching up my ankles, crawling it's way to my knees, and pounding against my chest until it found its home in my lung and yet somehow im not dead, although the thought that it would end carved it's name in the deepest recesses of my mind over and over incessantly marking its territory. Over time, hope made its conjugal visit in short phrases:

i want to breathe again,
i want to heal and mend.

~Davion Alexander

{ 13 }

Happy Ending or Just Beginning?

As a hopeless romantic, I loved the end of the movie or book that stated, "the end". It implied that everything would be ok, and everyone's life overcame whatever tragedy they harbored. Unfortunately, that was not the end of my story. I woke up just as confused as I had been for the last 15 years of my life. As I replayed the promise I made to the boys, I wondered how I would bring it to fruition. Because I didn't have a clear plan, I spent years of my life much of the same. My drinking habit continued to grow, and my relationship with men would change with the season. No one in my family was a help as they were all making messes of their lives while looking for me to clean it up. On top of that I had not learned money management, and while I was pretending to understand, I didn't. Although nothing was being cut off, I came closer more than not. D and Davion were in middle school, and I was trying to keep up with the rest of the children so they wouldn't feel left out. Something was missing that was causing the continuous recycling of self-disappointment.

Living in an atmosphere where your surroundings manipulate your life can be life damning. It will change the view you have of yourself and keep you from stepping into your position so that you can change your perception. Here I was doing the same thing with the same people, looking for and hoping for my life to change. After a few years, I decided it was time to make some real changes. I went to my boss and asked her what it would take for me to move up. Maybe if my professional life changed, it would pour over into my personal life. There was a problem: although I was great at my job, I was not liked. From the day Daniel went to prison, and I became a single mom, I blamed him for everything that went wrong in our lives. Although he wasn't perfect, he was the hedge of protection that was keeping them from being able to use me. Now that I was alone, they expected me to do the things I paid for for free. Over time, my resentment for them all began to spew out at work with management, causing stunted growth for myself. Jill and I had something in common: we were not liked, but our goal was to go as far as we could no matter what. She gave me advice that would grow me professionally but would belittle me personally. See, Jill understood the game, and she also understood the frustration I had with previous management. Their goal was to keep me talking, so they had reason for not promoting me, and I was playing right into their hands. Jill's advice was for me to swallow how I felt at work, scream when I got home, and get the promotions I deserved. No one was going to see my potential if all they heard was my mouth, so I did exactly what she recommended and before long I was moving in the right direction.

A year later, I was promoted to supervisor at one of the offices where I had previously worked. Here, I was overseeing people who despised me and working alongside people who didn't want to see me in my position. Every day was a constant struggle to keep the real me hidden so that I could keep my professional position of Supervisor. D, Davion, and Dimarrius were enjoying the fruits of my labor even though the stress was taking a toll on me. We were always doing something and taking trips, so I figured their smiles were all I needed to keep going. I heavily depended on Prozac and Xanax to keep me centered so that I wouldn't damper the lives the boys had become accustomed to. It was a very good fairytale, but in real life, I felt smothered by a version of myself that was constantly telling the real me I wasn't good enough. It didn't help that after 1 ½ years of giving this position all of me the AVP decided to say those words out loud and crush me. My manager decided to quit while I was on vacation at Disneyworld with my family, and I came back to take over his position. They praised me for my work to my face while criticizing me behind my back. I didn't know it until I was ready to step into the role and they told me I wasn't quite ready. The jealous employees I went from working with to supervising made sure they complained about the smallest things I didn't do for them. It didn't matter that all their quality measures had been met and I had changed; all they saw was the same person and that I didn't belong with them.

After playing my part of supporting the unqualified person they brought in to be my new manager, I walked away to a less stressful position with more money. I decided I had taken all I could and realized that this was as far as I would go under this management. Besides, it was 2015, and D was a senior in high school, so I had better things to put my time into. He and I had been back and forth about college, and although I wanted him to go, he showed me that school was not his favorite place. He was already in the new high school-college provided by CPCC and it was not fulfilling, so I was unsure how he would adapt. Just when I thought the decision was made that he wasn't going, Daniel called and convinced him that he should. This was just like him playing dad after all the hard work had been completed. All those thoughts went away when D was accepted into the school he wanted, East Carolina University. Even though I didn't know how I would pay for him to go, it wouldn't stop me from making sure he had what he needed. The fear that was holding me from being truly excited for my son was removed, and I was ready to send him off to college. As we drove him to the beginning of his adult life, I let him know that while I would always be there, this was his time to find himself. What I did not want for him was to become what I wanted and resent me for it. I understood what this did to a person, so when he left, my only requirement was he came home for the holidays.

As I was settling D in his first year of college, Davion began his last year of high school. The transition was not easy, but since I just finished this I had a road map of where to begin. Amid everything, Dimarrius was beginning to show signs of struggling to cope with middle school. Thankfully, my dear friend Susan told me about a job working from home which assisted me with maintaining all these moving parts. My professional life now had flexibility, allowing me to be present during school hours without thinking about the money or PTO I was losing. It also gave me time to think about my next move, which was to fix the discrepancies in my life and live how I was meant to live. After I weighed the pros and cons, I decided that Dimarrius and I would move in with my dad after Davion went to college. My goal was to fix my credit and buy a home. I didn't want anyone else to be able to tell me no about where I wanted to live. I was thrilled that Davion was accepted in UNC Chappel Hill on an academic scholarship. This removed the worry of how I could take care of two college students.

After we dropped D and Davion off at college, it was time to finish packing. My move-out date was September 1st, 2017, and there was plenty of work to do. My friend was there to help me get through the hard part, which was understanding that I wasn't losing anything but gaining the future I wanted. Once again, the perception of what people thought about me rang supreme in my mind, overshadowing what I wanted. I had held on to my place longer than any place on my own, and while I was proud of what I was able to accomplish, I was fearful of the future. What if I didn't get it right? What if I was making the wrong decision? It was too late to change my mind as it was moving day, and there was no turning back. My dad welcomed us with open arms, and while it was an adjustment for all of us, I was determined. For a year and a half, I worked 16 hours to pay off my debt while buying furniture for the day I no longer called my dad's place our home. It was hard taking off the rose-colored lenses of a child, hoping everything turns out like I want it, and develop the discipline I lacked for so long.

Our time there wasn't easy as my dad and I led very different lives, and I was not bending on mine. We fought sometimes but understood it was done in love. While I was accomplishing my goal of paying off debt and personal growth, the enemy saw it as an opportunity to slow me down. Dimarrius and I constantly fought over his grades and lack of concern as long as he could continue playing sports. I was getting headaches that were so bad that I would have to visit the ER for relief. When that didn't work, he attacked my health with a breast cancer scare that resulted in benign then my father with a kidney bleed that started in his slow but quick demise. Quickly, I started to believe that I had made the wrong decision and was being punished. My dad and I both ended up having to have surgery, and although I healed nicely, his healing took longer and was more trips back and forth to the ER. I figured I needed to stay longer so that I could get Dimarrius in line and make sure my dad was ok. Once again, my father had to remind me that I wasn't coming to stay but only passing through. Fear found itself present now that nothing was holding me back. The Holy Spirit also reminded me that I had nothing to fear as I wasn't alone in my next phase in life.

They were right, so I began looking for Dimarrius and I a place to call home. Originally, I wanted to move back to the South side but decided my life was now on the Northwest. This left me close enough to my family to be there but far enough that I wasn't so involved in how they lived their lives. I had allowed the lines to become so blurred over the years, and now my son needed me more than anyone. We settled on a nice two-bedroom two two-bath open concept apartment. Incidentally, they listed my apartment incorrectly but honored the original price even though I hadn't signed a lease. It was a new complex, so we had our pick of what we wanted and chose the biggest floor plan. Our apartment was where we could see the sun rise and set beautifully. Now that it was only the two of us, I decided on some off-white furniture with a white plush fur rug. It matched perfectly with the apartment as it was fully loaded with stainless-steel appliances. For the first time, my deposit was the minimum as my credit spoke for me. It was the week of Christmas 2018, and I decided my present to myself, and Dimarrius would be moving into our apartment.

As I looked around the apartment, I felt like I had finally arrived at my right place. The problem was when I left my last apartment, I told myself when I moved again, it would be into my own home. This would be my first home as the last one was in Daniel's name and never felt like home. It was as if I was living in protective custody and was forever looking over my shoulder. When I looked at this apartment, it was the same way. Since Daniel's release date was coming soon, I alienated myself from his family. The only person I trusted to see where I lived was his brother, and that was only once to get his hair done. Occasionally, I daydreamed about our many fights and was reluctant to deal with that part of Daniel again.

I didn't understand that Dimarrius felt like he was also living in a jail since he was losing contact with the friends he made in middle school. Although we attended church, more than not, it didn't seem like any of it was reaching him, and now here we were verbally fighting. Amid everything, I was trying to go back to school and get my degree. I had tried so many times before but, for one reason or another, stopped. Since only the two of us were there, I figured it was as good a time as ever. Before I could become too involved in school, a family emergency once again took me from my personal goals.

As Camila waited for her apartment to become available, she allowed my niece, Jazmine to live with me temporarily. Jazmine was the first and only girl in our family so far, whose birthday was two days after mine. She was always so full of life that I was always happy to have her around. There were two problems with her moving in that were beyond her control. One, I was dealing with Dimarrius and didn't feel I had the mental capacity to help anyone else, and two, I had told my boys years before that NO ONE else would be allowed to live with us. I had pushed them over to make room for someone else so many times that it made me sick. That's not to say they had not temporarily made room for us, but never while their children suffered. What was more hurtful is that none of them once said, "no, we'll sleep on the floor in the living room," until I said, "no, you will have to sleep on the floor in the living room and make it short-lived". While it wasn't Jazmines's fault, she was going to have to sleep in the living room. It hurt my heart to see, but I couldn't bear putting my son out of his room, and they were too old to sleep in the same room.

Once she was acclimated to how things went in our house, things were smooth sailing. To make sure I didn't lose touch with Dimarrius, I sent her to be with Camila on the weekends and teacher workdays so I could spend time with him. All I could do was hope it was making a difference as he was not a big talker, so I never knew what was truly bothering him to begin with. Nevertheless, I continued to go through the motions, hoping that one day, he would open up and tell me how I could help him.

While working with Dimarrius, I noticed that the affordable housing issue was gaining more attention but was still met with opposition. The apartments that we once called home and considered one of the best places to live on the west side had fallen to scum. They had changed management hands several times, and now this management was putting them out to remodel them. The problem was that when they were finished, they were raising the rent far beyond what the residents could afford. Quickly, I wanted to help but didn't know what to do. I called on some mentors from a program Davion and Dimarrius participated in to get some guidance, and before long, I was establishing a non-profit organization. Here I was hoping to save someone else when my door could have used some sweeping around. While I was planning and organizing, my father got sick again. It was an odd time in my life because I never thought about saving people outside of the people I was forced to help within my own family. I was able to organize my first event with my non-profit and was very proud of what I was doing. Although my dad wished he could be there, we went by the hospital after to wish him a happy birthday. Ben was never present when anyone needed him, so it didn't surprise me that he didn't attend either.

{ 14 }

Time to Face the Music

I left 2019 feeling pretty good about everything I was able to accomplish. My dad needed extra care, so I sent Jazmine home so I could take care of him. She was not happy, and it was understandable by living with me, she was finally able to be herself. Besides that, Camila had promised help that she neglected to give for fear that what she was doing was benefiting Dimarrius and me. It was the most irresponsible action by anyone receiving help, but I figured it was time she took full responsibility, and I took care of my own home.

It was a new year, and what I'd hoped was a better opportunity for all who lived to see it. Now it was time my dad returned the favor as I needed another surgery. It wasn't serious, but I thought it was necessary. When I got out of the hospital, I saw a message on my phone from Daniel's brother. We hadn't spoken since I told him I was no longer doing hair, so I was confused and curious about why he was calling me. As I listened to the message, I thought he was seriously playing a joke on me. "Hey Brandy, Daniel is out of prison and is trying to reach you," he said. I knew I would be forced to deal with my past one day, but I couldn't believe out of all the days it would be today. He had called Dimarrius a few weeks before, talking about looking for a halfway house and needing my help. To keep myself out of the mix, I gave the information to the boys, who asked if I could help. For them, I did, but he never called back to get the information from Dimarrius, so I thought nothing else of it.

As I returned the call to the number left for Daniel, I was fearful of what I would hear on the other end. Although I had grown personally, I had forgotten that I needed to heal from my past. I swept it under the rug with everything else wrong in my life, hoping it would disappear. Just like a new relationship, everything started fine, but we had too much baggage for things to stay calm. This time, it wasn't about us; it was all about the boys having a relationship with Daniel. I knew what it was like to grow up fatherless, so I was going to be the good girl so my children could work through that part of their lives. He asked if he could see the boys, and I said that was up to them.

D and Davion came home that week for spring break, and I let them decide to see him. When they returned crying hysterically, over-run by emotions, I let Daniel know he was not going to hurt them, or he would have to deal with me. Dimarrius internalized his emotions, and it was back to us having heated arguments. In March 2020, while I was planning another event, the world was struck with a pandemic that resulted in a lockdown. This meant D and Davion had to come home as colleges shut down and sent students home. In one month, my life shifted in an unfamiliar direction.

This was the last thing Dimarrius needed for a child already strug-gling emotionally. After continuous tries to help Dimarrius adjust, I figured it best he lived with Daniel for a while. My hope was that Daniel could give him the time he needed from a father and help him understand his choices if he continued on this path. I had never allowed anyone to speak into my children's lives, and now I was beg-ging for someone to save my son. As a mom, I had done and said all I knew to say or do.

As summer approached, I hoped Dimarrius would return, but he was hell-bent on proving me wrong, so he decided to stay with Daniel. Although I wasn't thrilled about the idea, I decided not to fight it. D was assigned to all online classes, so it was he and I for now. While

I could not reach Dimarrius at this time, D and I were able to get to know one another. It was the conversations we never knew we needed as mom and son, and I was glad for how it happened. As the government was relaxing the restrictions for going out, I rode past what was my new home. Unfortunately, I had ridden past this place time and time again and told myself I could never live there. Gave every excuse possible for the two years since the beginning of their building my new community.

One day, while my dad and I were out cruising, I asked him if he wanted to see something. He and I shared a lot, so I trusted his judgment at times. With butterflies in my stomach, I drove the route to get to the neighborhood and asked to see the model home. It was a gorgeous five-bedroom, three-bathroom home. Open floor plan, two car garage, with all appliances included. When they told me how much the home was, I figured there was no way I was going to be able to afford this home. Our first home was 106,000 with a 7.5% interest rate and payments of $866, and I had to foreclose. This home was $317,000, and I figured there was no way I could be approved or afford the payments.

They asked for a $1500 earnest payment that was non-refundable, so I went home and prayed. Although I had already been praying, I wanted to make sure I wasn't making a mistake. Sometimes, we tend to think we heard from God in order to advance our own agenda. At this time in my life, I cannot say that I truly heard from God to make this decision, but I prayed that if I didn't need this home, please not let the application be approved. However, I wanted this and worked so hard to get to this place. Interest rates were dropping because of the pandemic, but there was a catch: materials were increasing because of the pandemic and the lack of workers. As I completed the application and paid the fee, I was terrified of the results. When I received the approval, I was stunned. Although I made good money, I didn't think I deserved this, but I did. There was a catch that I had to say yes asap as housing prices were about to increase because of the rising price of materials. If that weren't enough, there was a guy who wanted the same home and wanted to start a bidding war. It was then that I said no, I'm not bidding for something that belongs to me. If I should have it, there would be no obstacles in my way. I completed every assignment they put before me, and my supporters were there to keep me motivated when I got distracted. While they projected me to close in November, I was ready in October. My dad went with me to sign my life away, as they put it when you are buying a home. When I pulled up to my new three-bedroom two-and-a-half bathroom and turned the key, I knew there was no mistake on what I received. This home was big enough just for me yet big enough for my family. It was a moment I'll never forget.

This was just in time for my first Thanksgiving and my first son graduating from college.

{ 15 }

The Last Act?

One thing about my life is the need to never give up. I have persevered through some of the hardest times in my life and mostly remained humble. I admit there were times when I wanted to and gloated about what I had accomplished. Obviously, 2020 was not the end of my life. It was the ending to the story about my life that I was willing to speak about. Although it ended on a high note, that wasn't realistic as to how the rest of my story went. Three years after buying my home, I lost my dad, severed my relationship with my immediate family and some who I called friends, started a podcast, and folded my business.

It was the hardest time of my life when I started to question my purpose for my life. I waited so long for my dad to come back, and right when I was getting started, he died, and a part of me died as well. As I tried to persevere, I kept falling and losing everything I considered important around me. Referring to a dream I had in December 2022, I interpreted it as something that has to die in order for you to live. In the beginning, I thought that was my father. He had become very ill, and I was his full-time caretaker. But when he passed, and the load hadn't lightened but only gotten heavier, I knew I was missing something.

Every time I turned around it was another obstacle, another loss, and staying optimistic was becoming impossible. Credit cards were maxed, money was low, and I had to go back to working for some-one else to make ends meet. Making my cell phone payments had become hard because of the amount of debt I was under. For the third time in my life, I considered suicide. While I was too embarrassed to admit my failures, I was descending deeper into depression. I began blaming myself for everything going wrong until I realized what the dream meant.

All my life, I have lived for everyone but myself. My family, career, hobbies, friends all came from someone telling me what I needed in my life as opposed to what we shared in life. I don't possess friendships that stem from years of building and molding unconditional love for one another. I don't possess family bonds, as I have been blessed and cursed by the tongue of those I used to hold near and dear. I don't possess a career that I enjoy getting up to work for daily. Lastly, I don't possess many hobbies because everything I've enjoyed has been to please someone else. This is not me complaining but merely stating facts that help you understand who I have been and why I had the dream.

In life, we are all dealt a hand. Now, some of us take that hand we are dealt and play it until we are worn down. Then there are those of us who understand that although we are dealt a ruthless hand, it doesn't mean we don't have options. God gives us the discernment to choose but it's up to us to use it. We must understand that he wants what's best for us, but it comes at a cost. That cost may include giving up what we consider near and dear to possess something better. That includes hatred, disappointment, regret, anger, betrayal, hurt, aban-donment, relationships, and anything else that keeps you in the same state of repetition. All these things keep you from seeing the bigger picture, and understanding life is more than just that one hand.

For me, I hung on to the losses in my life like the next breath in my lungs. My mind made me believe that it would be the last time I had whatever I lost. When asked, "Do you know how blessed you are?" I responded by saying, "I honestly don't think about it". I stayed so focused on what I lost that I couldn't see the gain. As I begin to see not where I came from to where I am but what I had as I went through, I understand how blessed I am. So, when I hear people boast about my fake rag to riches, pulled up by the bootstrap story I hope they see the blessing of my story. The healing that is taking place in my life is more important than the house I live in. The forgiveness I have for myself and others is worth more than the trips I take. And while I continue trying to possess those blessings, I hope I see that I was never meant to be perfect...

I was meant to never give up!

Brandy Alexander was born and raised in Charlotte, NC. A single, parent of three, her goal is break generational curses and improve mental health. Brandy's parents separated when she was eight which left her broken. After experiencing mental abuse from her mom and abandonment from her dad, Brandy turned to a life of alcohol, drugs, and sexual relationships. This led her to poor decision making and a mother of two by the age of 17. She met what would become her husband at the age of 14 who abused her mentally, emotionally and physically until the age 26. Her life since has been a journey to overcome the trauma from all her obstacles. At 22, Brandy managed to get her GED, 28 get a divorce, and by 42 decided it was time to take back her life. Brandy is the founder of a non profit that assists at risk youth from becoming a statistic, an author, public speaker and a believer of God.

Davion Alexander is a NC based poet, born and raised in Charlotte, NC. He attended the University of North Carolina at Chapel Hill where he studied biology with a pre-med focus. Throughout his college career, he would begin to dive into the world of poetry as a mechanism for healing. The poems were Christian focused as it reflected his thoughts and beliefs at the time but once he graduated and began to dive into his sexuality, childhood, and his identity outside of religion, these poems began to reflect the mind of a black queer artist coming into his own. Since then, he has created an on-line Instagram profile to showcase his poems and has performed at several open mic nights in the Raleigh, NC area with the hope of one day publishing several books of poetry.